Table of Contents

01: The Journey to Effortless Progress 2

02: The Science of Small Wins 12

03: Building Sustainable Habits with Micro-Goals 20

04: The Power of Essentialism 28

05: Simplifying Decision-Making for Effortless Progress 38

06: Mastering Time: How to Make the Most of Every Moment 45

07: Navigating Common Obstacles on the Path to Effortless Progress 54

08: The Power of Systems: Creating Structures that Lead to Progress 63

09: Sustaining Effortless Progress: Building a Life of Simplicity and Achievement 75

10: Further Reading and Academic References 84

01: The Journey to Effortless Progress

In today's fast-paced world, we're often told that the key to success is to hustle—to work harder, push longer, and fill every waking moment with productivity. Our calendars are bursting with meetings, tasks, and goals, while our to-do lists never seem to get shorter. We move from one commitment to the next, constantly busy but rarely feeling accomplished.

But here's the hard truth: being busy is not the same as being productive.

While many of us spend our days in constant motion, we're not necessarily moving toward the things that truly matter. The endless hustle, while glorified in popular culture, often leads to burnout, stress, and a feeling of being stuck in place. Despite all the effort, progress feels elusive, like trying to run up a never-ending hill.

In fact, a study from Stanford University found that productivity per hour declines sharply when a person works more than 50 hours per week. After 55 hours, productivity drops so much that working any more hours becomes practically pointless. This research reveals that overwork doesn't equate to greater output—if anything, it leads to diminishing returns.

What if it didn't have to be this way? What if success didn't require you to exhaust yourself or constantly struggle to keep up? What if progress could feel natural, smooth, and—dare I say—effortless?

That's what this book is about: showing you how to make progress in your life, career, and personal goals without constantly burning yourself out. It's about embracing simplicity, building systems that work for you, and learning to flow toward your goals with greater ease and less resistance.

Effortless progress is not about taking shortcuts or avoiding hard work. Instead, it's about aligning your efforts with what truly matters, focusing on the right things, and creating sustainable habits that support long-term success. When you learn to make progress effortlessly, you're no longer fighting against the tide; instead, you're harnessing it to propel you forward.

The Myth of Hustle Culture

We've been taught that success comes only through grinding, sacrificing sleep, and constantly pushing ourselves beyond our limits. This mindset, often referred to as "hustle culture," tells us that if we're not working harder than everyone else, we're falling behind. But this relentless pursuit of productivity can be toxic.

The truth is hustle culture doesn't lead to lasting success—it leads to exhaustion.

Research published in the journal *Sleep* has shown that chronic sleep deprivation, which is common in those trying to "hustle" their way to success, impairs cognitive performance, creativity, and problem-solving abilities. Sleep-deprived individuals are more prone to making mistakes, experiencing burnout, and struggling with decision-making. Essentially, the very approach that's meant to help you achieve more may be preventing you from reaching your full potential.

Take a moment to reflect on this: How often have you found yourself working late into the night, feeling burned out but without a sense of accomplishment? Have you ever noticed how, despite checking off tasks from your to-do list, you still feel like you're not getting anywhere?

Hustle culture glorifies busyness, not effectiveness. It convinces us that working more equals success, but in reality, it's often the opposite. When we overextend ourselves without clear direction or purpose, we sacrifice the very elements that lead to meaningful progress: focus, energy, and creativity.

Case Study: The Story of John

John was a rising executive in a fast-paced tech startup. Like many, he believed that working longer hours and keeping his schedule packed would eventually lead to a promotion and a sense of fulfilment. He was the first in the office and often the last to leave, always juggling multiple projects. His calendar was filled with back-to-back meetings, and his inbox never seemed to reach zero.

But despite the hustle, John wasn't making significant progress toward his long-term goals. He felt trapped in a cycle of busyness without a sense of real achievement. The constant juggling left him feeling mentally drained, and the more he worked, the less time he had to reflect, plan, or recharge.

John's breakthrough came when he learned to adopt the principles of effortless progress. He realized that his success wasn't about doing more; it was about doing what mattered most. By cutting out unnecessary meetings, delegating tasks that weren't critical to his role, and using systems to streamline his workday, he found that he could accomplish more in fewer hours.

John's life transformed. Not only did his productivity increase, but he also had more time for family, hobbies, and rest. He no longer needed to work 60-hour weeks to feel successful. Instead, he achieved effortless progress by focusing on simplicity, priorities, and strategic effort.

John's story is a perfect example of the contrast between hustle culture and effortless progress. It shows that lasting success isn't about how much you do—it's about the quality and focus of your efforts.

The Core Promise of This Book

This book will guide you on a journey toward effortless progress. Throughout its chapters, you'll learn how to create a life where success feels simple and achievable, not overwhelming. You'll discover how to design systems that allow you to make steady progress without relying on constant motivation, and how to simplify your decision-making process so that you can focus your mental energy on what matters most.

By the end of this book, you'll have the tools to:
- **Create systems that automate your success**: Whether in your career, health, or personal life, you'll learn to set up systems that streamline your actions and make progress inevitable.
- **Build habits that last**: Instead of relying on willpower and discipline, you'll build habits that become part of your everyday routine, allowing you to achieve your goals with minimal effort.
- **Master your time**: You'll learn how to manage your time effectively, structuring your day around your most important tasks and eliminating time-wasting distractions.
- **Simplify your life**: We'll explore strategies for reducing complexity in your decisions, routines, and commitments, allowing you to focus on the activities that drive real results.
- **Achieve sustainable growth**: The key to long-term success is not short bursts of intense effort but steady, consistent progress. You'll learn how to sustain your efforts over the long haul without burning out.

At its core, this book is about teaching you how to create progress that feels natural—where your actions align with your goals, and where your systems and habits carry you forward with less effort.

Why Simplicity Works

Simplicity is the foundation of effortless progress. When we overcomplicate things—whether it's our workday, our goals, or our daily decisions—we waste mental energy and create unnecessary stress. Simplicity, on the other hand, brings clarity. It allows you to focus on what's truly important and eliminates the distractions that pull you off course.

The Science Behind Simplicity

Research shows that humans have a limited amount of cognitive resources to make decisions each day. A study by psychologist Roy Baumeister and his colleagues found that decision-making depletes mental energy and self-control, a phenomenon known as *decision fatigue*. The more decisions we make, the harder it becomes to focus, which leads to poor choices, procrastination, or even avoidance of decisions altogether.

Simplicity helps counteract decision fatigue by minimizing the number of trivial choices we face each day. By automating repetitive decisions—such as what to eat, what to wear, or how to manage routine tasks—we free up mental space for more important matters. This is why successful individuals like Steve Jobs and Mark Zuckerberg are known for wearing the same types of clothing daily. They understood that eliminating small decisions allowed them to focus their energy on higher-priority tasks.

The Power of Focus

Consider the difference between a laser and a floodlight. A floodlight disperses light over a wide area, illuminating everything but with less intensity. A laser, however, concentrates its light into a narrow beam, allowing it to cut through even the toughest materials. The same principle applies to your efforts. When you focus your energy on too many things at once, you dilute your effectiveness. But when you concentrate your efforts on a few high-impact activities, you can achieve far more with less effort.

A Practical Example of Focus

Let's take the example of Sarah, a marketing professional who found herself overwhelmed by the sheer number of projects she had to manage. Each day, she was pulled in multiple directions—meetings with clients, brainstorming sessions, administrative work, and responding to endless emails. Sarah was spread too thin, and her productivity suffered as a result.

Recognizing that she needed to regain control of her workload, Sarah adopted a new approach based on the principles of effortless progress. She began by simplifying her workday. Instead of trying to juggle every task simultaneously, she started focusing on her highest-priority tasks first. She used time blocking to dedicate specific hours of the day to deep work and reserved other times for less demanding tasks like answering emails or attending meetings.

By simplifying her focus and eliminating unnecessary distractions, Sarah saw a dramatic improvement in her productivity. She was able to complete her most important projects faster, with higher quality, and without feeling constantly stressed or overwhelmed.

The power of focus lies in its ability to cut through distractions and allow you to work on the things that matter most. When you focus on fewer, more meaningful tasks, you create a greater impact with less effort.

Key Themes of Effortless Progress

Effortless progress is built on several core principles, each of which we'll explore in depth throughout the book. These principles form the foundation of a life where progress feels easy and sustainable.

1. Simplifying Decision-Making

Every day, we're faced with a barrage of decisions—what to wear, what to eat, what to work on, and how to prioritize our time. Each decision, no matter how small, takes up mental energy. This is known as *decision fatigue*, and it's one of the main reasons why people struggle to stay focused and make consistent progress.

In the chapters ahead, you'll learn how to simplify your decision-making process by creating routines and systems that eliminate unnecessary choices. By automating certain aspects of your life—like meal planning, daily scheduling, and task prioritization—you'll free up mental energy to focus on the decisions that truly matter.

For example, successful leaders like Mark Zuckerberg and Barack Obama have been known to streamline their wardrobes, wearing the same or similar outfits every day to minimize trivial decisions. This seemingly small habit frees up mental space for more critical decisions.

2. Mastering Time Management

Time is our most valuable resource, yet many of us feel like we never have enough of it. The problem isn't the amount of time we have but how we use it. Effortless progress requires mastering the art of time management—learning how to structure your day around your priorities, eliminate time-wasting activities, and protect your focus.

This book will introduce you to powerful time management strategies, such as time blocking and the Pomodoro technique, that help you make the most of every moment. You'll also learn how to create a daily rhythm that supports your goals and allows you to make steady progress without feeling rushed or overwhelmed.

Research published in the *Harvard Business Review* has shown that individuals who block out uninterrupted time for focused work are significantly more productive than those who constantly multitask. Time blocking—where specific times are reserved for deep, focused work—has proven to enhance concentration and boost output.

3. Building Systems for Success

Systems are the secret to achieving consistent progress without relying on willpower or motivation. A system is a set of repeatable actions that drive results automatically. When you have a system in place, progress becomes inevitable because the system does the work for you.

Throughout this book, we'll explore how to create systems that support your most important goals. Whether you want to improve your health, grow your career, or strengthen your relationships, building the right systems will ensure that you're always moving forward, even on the days when motivation is low.

4. Creating Long-Lasting Habits

Habits are the building blocks of your success. Once a habit is established, it becomes automatic—something you do without thinking. The challenge, of course, is building habits that last. Many people struggle to stick with new habits because they rely too heavily on willpower, which inevitably fades over time.

In the pages ahead, you'll learn how to build habits that stick by starting small, using habit stacking, and creating triggers that make it easier to stay consistent. You'll also discover how to recover from setbacks and avoid the trap of perfectionism, so that one slip-up doesn't derail your progress.

A Personal Story: Simplifying for Success

Years ago, I found myself caught in the same cycle that many people experience. I was constantly busy, always hustling, and trying to do it all. I believed that the key to success was working harder than everyone else, so I filled my days with meetings, tasks, and projects, rarely stopping to rest or reflect.

But despite all my effort, I wasn't making the progress I wanted. I was moving in too many directions at once, constantly juggling competing priorities. It felt like I was spinning my wheels—busy, but not productive.

That's when I realized I needed a change. I began by simplifying my life, focusing on fewer goals, and building systems that allowed me to make steady progress without burning myself out. I created routines that supported my most important tasks, and I learned to let go of the things that weren't truly necessary.

The difference was immediate and profound. By focusing on simplicity and building systems, I was able to accomplish more in less time. My stress levels decreased, my productivity soared, and I finally felt in control of my progress.

This shift didn't happen overnight, and it required me to rethink the way I approached work and success. But once I embraced the principles of effortless progress, everything became easier.

Your First Step: Simplifying Your Life

As you begin this journey toward effortless progress, I encourage you to start by simplifying one area of your life. What's one task, decision, or routine that feels unnecessarily complicated? Maybe it's your morning routine, your work schedule, or how you manage your personal goals.

Take a moment to reflect on how you could simplify this area. Could you streamline a daily task, automate a decision, or eliminate something that's no longer serving you? Simplifying just one part of your day will give you a taste of how powerful simplicity can be.

This small step is the beginning of a much larger transformation. As you read through the following chapters, you'll learn how to apply the principles of simplicity, systems, and habits to every aspect of your life. You'll discover how to create lasting progress that feels natural and effortless.

Conclusion

Effortless progress is about creating a life where success feels achievable and sustainable. It's not about working harder or doing more—it's about focusing on what truly matters, simplifying your approach, and building systems that support long-term growth.

Throughout this book, you'll learn practical strategies for mastering decision-making, time management, and habit formation. You'll build systems that make progress automatic and develop habits that stick for the long haul.

This journey won't require you to hustle harder or push yourself to the brink. Instead, it will show you how to align your actions with your goals in a way that feels natural and rewarding. With the right mindset, strategies, and systems, you'll find that progress becomes effortless.

Welcome to the path of effortless progress.

02: The Science of Small Wins

Introduction: Why Small Wins Matter More Than You Think

When working toward a big goal, it's easy to become fixated on the end result. Whether it's losing 50 pounds, writing a book, or earning a promotion, the finish line often feels so far away that we forget to focus on the smaller achievements along the way. This focus on the end result can lead to frustration and burnout when progress feels slow.

However, research shows that **small wins**—those minor but consistent achievements we make along the way—are incredibly powerful motivators. These small victories create a sense of momentum and provide the positive reinforcement needed to stay motivated and committed to long-term goals.

The concept of small wins was popularized by **Teresa Amabile**, a professor at Harvard Business School, whose research found that even the smallest steps forward significantly improve motivation and performance. In this chapter, we'll explore the psychology of small wins, why they are crucial to long-term success, and how you can harness their power in your daily life.

The Psychology Behind Small Wins: How Progress Fuels Motivation

At the core of small wins is the psychological principle that **progress is motivating**. When we see ourselves making progress, no matter how small, our brain releases **dopamine**, a neurotransmitter associated with pleasure and reward. This dopamine hit reinforces the behavior that led to the progress, making us more likely to repeat it.

This phenomenon is backed by research. **Teresa Amabile's study** of nearly 12,000 daily work diaries found that employees who made even minor progress on their tasks reported higher levels of engagement and job satisfaction than those who didn't experience progress. The small wins, not the major breakthroughs, had the most significant impact on their motivation.

This same principle applies to personal goals. Whether you're aiming to build a new habit, learn a skill, or improve your health, the sense of accomplishment from a small win keeps you motivated to continue.

Example:
Consider someone trying to build the habit of exercising regularly. Instead of setting a lofty goal to exercise for an hour each day, they might set a smaller goal to walk for 10 minutes. Each day they complete their 10-minute walk, they experience a small win—a feeling of success that makes it easier to stick to the routine and eventually build up to longer workouts.

Why Small Wins Are So Powerful: The Compound Effect

The impact of small wins isn't just about the immediate reward. Over time, these small wins compound, leading to significant results. This is often referred to as the **compound effect**, a concept explored in depth by **Darren Hardy** in his book *The Compound Effect*. Hardy explains that small, seemingly insignificant actions, when repeated consistently, can produce massive long-term outcomes.

The compound effect is like planting a seed. Each small win is a drop of water that helps the seed grow. At first, the growth is barely noticeable, but with consistent watering (small wins), the seed eventually blooms into a tree (the larger goal).

Example:
Imagine you're trying to save $10,000 in a year. Saving that amount all at once might seem impossible, but by setting a small win of saving $10 a day, you're steadily working toward the larger goal. After 100 days, you've already saved $1,000, and the progress keeps you motivated to continue. These small wins compound into a substantial sum over time.

How to Identify and Celebrate Small Wins

One of the keys to leveraging small wins is recognizing them. Too often, we downplay our achievements, focusing only on what's left to do rather than acknowledging how far we've come. By identifying and celebrating small wins, we reinforce the behaviors that lead to success and maintain our momentum.

Step 1: Break Your Goals into Micro-Steps

The first step in identifying small wins is breaking your larger goals into smaller, actionable steps, as discussed in Chapter 1. These micro-steps serve as the building blocks for your progress, and each one you complete represents a small win.

Example:
If your goal is to learn a new language, break it down into daily micro-steps, such as learning 5 new vocabulary words a day. Each time you complete this micro-goal, it's a small win that moves you closer to fluency.

Step 2: Track Your Progress

Tracking your progress is essential for recognizing small wins. Without a system in place to monitor your achievements, it's easy to overlook how much progress you've made. Whether you use a habit tracker, a journal, or an app, tracking your small wins gives you a visual reminder of your progress.

Example:
Let's say you're trying to write a book. Set a micro-goal to write 200 words a day and track each day you hit that goal. After a month, you'll have written 6,000 words—a significant chunk of your book. Seeing this progress in your tracker serves as a powerful motivator to keep going.

Step 3: Celebrate Each Win

Celebrating small wins reinforces the behavior that led to them. This doesn't mean throwing a party every time you complete a micro-goal, but it does mean taking a moment to acknowledge and reward yourself. Celebrations could be as simple as giving yourself a mental high-five, sharing your success with a friend, or treating yourself to something small.

Example:

If you've reached a milestone in your fitness journey, such as exercising consistently for 30 days, reward yourself with something meaningful, like a new piece of workout gear or a day off to relax. This celebration signals to your brain that the effort was worthwhile and encourages you to keep going.

The Role of Reflection in Building on Small Wins

While celebrating small wins is crucial, so is reflecting on them. Reflection allows you to recognize patterns, adjust your strategies, and gain insights into what's working and what isn't.

Weekly Reflection:

Set aside time each week to reflect on your progress. Ask yourself questions like:

- What small wins did I achieve this week?
- How did those wins make me feel?
- What challenges did I face, and how did I overcome them?
- What can I do next week to build on these wins?

Monthly Reflection:

At the end of each month, look back on the small wins you've accumulated. Notice how they've added up to significant progress toward your larger goal. Use this reflection to set new micro-goals for the upcoming month and to make any necessary adjustments to your strategy.

Example:

Let's say you've been working on improving your diet by adding more vegetables to your meals. At the end of the month, reflect on how many meals included vegetables, how you felt after eating them, and whether this small win has become part of your routine. If you find that you struggled to stick with the habit, reflect on what barriers you faced and how you can adjust your approach (e.g., meal prepping or experimenting with different vegetables).

Case Studies: How Small Wins Lead to Big Success

To further illustrate the power of small wins, let's look at real-life examples of individuals who have used this strategy to achieve significant success.

Case Study 1: Sarah's Weight Loss Journey

Sarah, a 45-year-old teacher, had struggled with weight loss for years. She had tried various diets and exercise programs but found it hard to stay consistent. Frustrated with her lack of progress, Sarah decided to take a different approach. Instead of focusing on losing 50 pounds, she set a micro-goal to lose just 1 pound each week.

Each week, Sarah focused on making small, sustainable changes, such as swapping soda for water and walking for 20 minutes after dinner. Every time she lost a pound, she celebrated the small win by treating herself to a new book or a fun outing. These small victories kept her motivated, and within a year, she had lost 52 pounds—surpassing her original goal.

Case Study 2: John's Career Advancement

John, a software engineer, wanted to advance in his career but felt stuck in his current role. Rather than trying to overhaul his entire career at once, John set a small win goal: to spend 15 minutes each day learning a new coding language.

Each day he completed his 15-minute learning session, he tracked his progress and acknowledged the small win. After three months, John had developed a new skill set and applied for a higher-level position at his company. The small, daily wins of consistent learning had compounded into a significant career advancement.

Case Study 3: Emily's Writing Habit

Emily, a 29-year-old aspiring writer, struggled to finish her novel. The idea of writing an entire book felt overwhelming, and she often procrastinated. To combat this, Emily set a micro-goal to write just 100 words a day—something small enough that it didn't feel intimidating.

Each day she hit her word count; she celebrated the small win by checking it off her habit tracker. Over time, these small wins built her confidence and made writing a daily habit. After a year, Emily had finished the first draft of her novel.

How to Apply the Science of Small Wins in Different Areas of Life

Small wins can be applied to any goal or area of life, from health and fitness to personal development and career growth. The key is to break down your goals into small, manageable actions that you can complete consistently.

Health and Fitness

In health and fitness, small wins are especially powerful because progress can often feel slow. By setting micro-goals like walking for 10 minutes a day, drinking more water, or eating one healthy meal a day, you create a sense of accomplishment that keeps you motivated.

Example:
If your goal is to run a marathon, start by setting a small win of running for 5 minutes a day. Each day you complete this micro-goal, it reinforces the habit, making it easier to increase your distance over time.

Career Growth

Career advancement often requires learning new skills, building relationships, or taking on new responsibilities. Small wins in this area could include completing one module of an online course each week, sending a networking email, or leading a small project.

Example:
If your goal is to get a promotion, set a small win to complete 15 minutes of leadership training each day. Over time, these small wins will build your skill set and position you for advancement.

Personal Development

Whether you're trying to build mindfulness, improve emotional intelligence, or pursue a new hobby, small wins help you stay consistent. These wins could include meditating for 5 minutes, reading one chapter of a personal development book, or practicing a new hobby for 10 minutes.

Example:
If your goal is to improve mindfulness, set a small win of meditating for 2 minutes a day. This small, achievable goal helps you build consistency, and over time, you can increase the duration as meditation becomes part of your routine.

How to Build Long-Term Success with Small Wins

Small wins are not just about the immediate boost in motivation—they're about creating long-term, sustainable success. By focusing on small, consistent actions, you build habits that last.

Here's how to ensure your small wins lead to long-term success:

1. **Stay Consistent**: The power of small wins lies in their consistency. Commit to your micro-goals every day, even when you don't feel like it. The more consistent you are, the more these small actions will become automatic habits.
2. **Adjust as Needed**: As you make progress, your goals may evolve. Be willing to adjust your micro-goals as

you grow. If a particular strategy isn't working, make a small adjustment and keep moving forward.
3. **Keep Tracking**: Continue tracking your small wins to maintain accountability and motivation. The visual reminder of your progress will keep you focused and motivated to keep going.

Conclusion: Harness the Power of Small Wins for Big Results

The science of small wins shows us that we don't need to wait for big, life-changing moments to feel successful. Instead, by focusing on small, incremental achievements, we build the momentum and motivation needed to reach our larger goals.

As you move forward on your journey, remember that progress doesn't have to be massive to be meaningful. Each small win brings you one step closer to success, and over time, those small steps add up to big results.

03: Building Sustainable Habits with Micro-Goals

Introduction: The Power of Habits in Achieving Long-Term Success

Habits are the foundation of much of what we do. They dictate how we spend our mornings, how we approach work, and even how we take care of our health. According to **Dr. Wendy Wood**, a leading researcher on habit formation, about **43% of daily actions** are driven by habits rather than conscious decision-making. This means that nearly half of what we do each day is automatic—driven by routines we've developed over time.

If you're aiming to achieve long-term success in any area of your life, from health to career to personal growth, building **sustainable habits** is key. But how do you ensure that these habits stick? The answer lies in the power of **micro-goals**—small, achievable steps that make habit formation easier and more sustainable.

In this chapter, we'll explore how micro-goals can help you build habits that last, the science behind habit formation, and strategies to turn these micro-goals into long-term, sustainable habits that support your personal and professional growth.

Why Habits Are So Important for Long-Term Success

It's often said that success isn't about what you do once in a while, but what you do consistently. Habits are what allow you to take consistent action toward your goals without relying on willpower or motivation. Once a behavior becomes a habit, it no longer feels like a chore—it becomes a part of your daily routine.

According to **Charles Duhigg**, author of *The Power of Habit*, habits follow a three-step loop:

1. **Cue**: A trigger that signals your brain to start a behavior.
2. **Routine**: The behavior itself, such as exercising, reading, or eating a healthy meal.
3. **Reward**: A positive reinforcement that tells your brain the behavior is worth remembering.

The more you repeat this habit loop, the more automatic the behavior becomes. Over time, habits free up mental energy, allowing you to focus on more complex tasks while the habit runs on autopilot.

The challenge, however, is in building habits that last. This is where micro-goals come in.

The Role of Micro-Goals in Habit Formation

Micro-goals are small, specific actions that are easy to accomplish. When it comes to habit formation, micro-goals are incredibly powerful because they make the behavior feel manageable and achievable, even on days when motivation is low.

Breaking down a habit into micro-goals reduces the mental resistance to starting the behavior. Each micro-goal feels so small that it doesn't require a lot of effort or willpower to complete, which makes it more likely that you'll stick with the habit over time.

Example:
Let's say you want to build the habit of exercising regularly, but the idea of working out for 30 minutes every day feels overwhelming. Instead of focusing on a full workout, set a micro-goal to do just 5 minutes of exercise each morning. This small, manageable goal reduces the mental resistance to starting, and once you've completed your 5 minutes, you'll often feel motivated to keep going.

The beauty of micro-goals is that they create momentum. Once you've started the behavior, it becomes easier to continue, and over time, these small wins build the foundation for a sustainable habit.

The Science Behind Habit Formation: Why Micro-Goals Work

The science of habit formation reveals why micro-goals are so effective in building lasting habits. According to **Dr. BJ Fogg**, a behavior scientist at Stanford University, successful habit formation depends on three factors:

1. **Motivation**: Your desire to perform the behavior.
2. **Ability**: Your capacity to perform the behavior.
3. **Prompt**: The trigger that cues the behavior.

Dr. Fogg's **Tiny Habits** method emphasizes that when motivation is low, the key to maintaining a habit is to make the behavior easier by reducing the effort required. This is where micro-goals come in. By making the behavior so small and easy that it doesn't require much motivation, you increase the likelihood of consistency.

Research Insight:

A study published in the **European Journal of Social Psychology** found that it takes an average of **66 days** for a new behavior to become automatic. However, the complexity of the behavior plays a significant role. Simpler behaviors (like drinking a glass of water in the morning) become automatic faster than more complex ones (like exercising for 30 minutes a day).

By starting with micro-goals, you simplify the behavior, which speeds up the process of habit formation. Over time, as the behavior becomes automatic, you can gradually increase the complexity of the habit.

How to Use Micro-Goals to Build Sustainable Habits

Now that we understand the science behind why micro-goals work, let's explore how to use them to build habits that last.

Step 1: Identify the Habit You Want to Build

The first step in building a habit with micro-goals is to identify the specific behavior you want to make a part of your routine. Be as clear and specific as possible. Instead of saying, "I want to get healthier," a more specific habit goal would be, "I want to walk for 10 minutes every morning."

Being specific makes it easier to create a micro-goal that aligns with your habit.

Step 2: Break the Habit into Micro-Steps

Once you've identified the habit, break it down into **micro-steps**—small, specific actions you can take each day to reinforce the behavior.

Example:
If your goal is to build the habit of reading more, a micro-goal could be to read just one page a day. This goal is so small and easy that it doesn't require a lot of time or effort, but it helps you build the habit of reading regularly.

Over time, you can gradually increase the number of pages you read each day, but the key is to start with a micro-goal that feels manageable.

Step 3: Tie the Habit to an Existing Routine

One of the most effective ways to build a new habit is to **tie it to an existing habit**—a concept known as **habit stacking**. This strategy involves using a habit you already perform as the cue for your new habit.

Example:
If you want to build the habit of meditating every day, stack it onto an existing habit, such as brushing your teeth in the morning. Your micro-goal could be to meditate for just 2 minutes after brushing your teeth. By linking the new habit to something you already do, you create a reliable trigger that makes the habit easier to remember.

Step 4: Track Your Progress

Tracking your progress is essential for building sustainable habits. Whether you use a habit tracker, journal, or app, tracking allows you to see how consistent you've been and reinforces the habit.

Example:
If your goal is to drink more water, use a water tracking app or a simple habit tracker to mark off each day you meet your micro-goal (e.g., drinking 8 glasses of water). Seeing your streak grow can be a powerful motivator to keep going.

Step 5: Celebrate Small Wins

Each time you complete a micro-goal, take a moment to celebrate the small win. Celebrating these wins reinforces the behavior and makes you more likely to repeat it.

Example:
If your goal is to exercise regularly, celebrate each time you complete your micro-goal (e.g., 5 minutes of exercise). This could be as simple as giving yourself a mental pat on the back or rewarding yourself with a healthy treat at the end of the week.

Case Studies: Real-Life Examples of Building Sustainable Habits with Micro-Goals

Let's look at a few real-life examples of how micro-goals can lead to lasting habits.

Case Study 1: Building a Fitness Habit

Maria, a 35-year-old accountant, had always struggled to stick with an exercise routine. Every time she set a goal to work out for 30 minutes a day, she would lose motivation within a few weeks. Instead of giving up, Maria decided to try a different approach by setting a micro-goal to do just 5 minutes of exercise each morning.

The 5-minute goal felt manageable, even on busy days. Over time, Maria found that she often wanted to exercise for longer than 5 minutes once she got started. After three months, she had built a consistent fitness habit, and her workouts had naturally extended to 30 minutes.

Case Study 2: Building a Reading Habit

John, a 42-year-old lawyer, wanted to build a habit of reading more books but found it hard to make time for reading in his busy schedule. He set a micro-goal to read just one page a night before bed. This small goal took less than a minute to complete, but it helped him build the habit of reading daily.

After a few weeks, John found himself reading more than one page most nights, and by the end of the year, he had finished 12 books. The micro-goal of reading just one page had turned reading into a consistent habit.

Case Study 3: Building a Journaling Habit

Emily, a 28-year-old teacher, wanted to start journaling as a way to reduce stress and reflect on her day. However, the thought of writing a full journal entry every night felt overwhelming. She set a micro-goal to write just one sentence in her journal before bed.

This small goal felt easy to accomplish, and over time, Emily found herself writing more than one sentence on most nights. The micro-goal helped her build a journaling habit that became a regular part of her evening routine.

Overcoming Challenges in Habit Formation

Building sustainable habits isn't always easy, and there will be days when you face challenges. The key is to anticipate these challenges and have strategies in place to overcome them.

Challenge 1: Lack of Motivation

There will be days when motivation is low, and the habit feels harder to complete. This is where micro-goals are especially useful. By making the goal so small that it doesn't require much motivation, you increase the likelihood of sticking with the habit even on difficult days.

Strategy:
On days when motivation is low, focus on completing the micro-goal, no matter how small. Even if you only do 5 minutes of exercise or read one page, you're still making progress.

Challenge 2: Life Disruptions

Unexpected events—like travel, illness, or a busy work schedule—can disrupt your routine and make it harder to stick with a habit.

Strategy:
When life gets in the way, adjust your micro-goal to fit your current situation. If you're traveling and can't do your regular workout, set a micro-goal to do 5 minutes of stretching in your hotel room. The key is to maintain consistency, even if the habit looks different.

Challenge 3: Boredom or Plateau

After a while, it's natural to feel bored with a habit or to hit a plateau where progress slows. This can lead to frustration or a loss of interest in the habit.

Strategy:
When boredom sets in, find ways to change up the habit or increase the challenge slightly. If you're bored with your current workout routine, try a new exercise or increase the intensity. If you've hit a plateau with your progress, adjust your micro-goal to add a new element that keeps you engaged.

How to Evolve Your Habits Over Time

As you become more consistent with your micro-goals, your habits will naturally evolve. What once felt like a challenge will become easier, and you may find that you're ready to increase the complexity or intensity of the habit.

Gradually Increase the Challenge:

Once a habit feels automatic, consider increasing the challenge by adjusting your micro-goals. For example, if you've been walking for 10 minutes a day, you might increase it to 15 minutes. The key is to make small, incremental changes that feel manageable.

Add New Habits:

As you master one habit, you can begin stacking new habits onto your routine. For example, if you've built a consistent habit of meditating for 5 minutes after brushing your teeth, you could add a new habit, like drinking a glass of water, to follow your meditation.

Track Long-Term Progress:

Continue tracking your habits over the long term to see how they evolve. Reflect on how far you've come, and celebrate the consistency you've built.

Conclusion: Building Habits That Last with Micro-Goals

The power of habits lies in their consistency, and micro-goals are the key to making that consistency achievable. By breaking down habits into small, manageable actions, you reduce the mental resistance to starting and create a foundation for long-term success.

As you continue your journey of building habits, remember that progress doesn't have to be massive to be meaningful. Each small action you take adds up over time, and before you know it, those micro-goals will have transformed into lasting habits that support your personal and professional growth.

04: The Power of Essentialism

We live in a time when our days are filled with endless tasks, opportunities, and distractions. It seems like there's always something new demanding our attention—emails to respond to, meetings to attend, or new goals to chase. But in this whirlwind of activity, the most important question we need to ask ourselves is: *Are we actually making progress?* The hard truth is, many of us are caught in the trap of being busy without being productive. We're constantly moving, but not necessarily moving closer to what really matters.

The solution to this problem is something both profound and simple: essentialism. At its core, essentialism is the practice of focusing on what is most important and eliminating the rest. It's the idea that, instead of trying to do everything, we do fewer things better. By doing less, we actually achieve more.

Why Focus Is the Key to Effortless Progress

The reason essentialism is so powerful is that it taps into one of the fundamental truths about progress: not all efforts are created equal. In fact, most of the things we do on a daily basis have little to no impact on our long-term success. It's easy to feel productive when we're crossing items off a to-do list, but are those tasks moving us closer to our goals?

When we look closely, we realize that most of what we do is busywork—tasks that keep us occupied but don't contribute much to meaningful progress. The key to effortless progress lies in identifying and focusing on the few tasks that truly matter—the ones that create the most impact with the least effort.

Let's think about this in terms of our personal lives. Consider the person who spends hours every day responding to emails, attending meetings, and putting out fires at work. They feel busy, even overwhelmed, but at the end of the day, they haven't made significant progress on their most important projects. Now compare that to someone who spends just a few hours a day, but those hours are laser-focused on their highest priorities. The second person is far more likely to make meaningful progress, even though they're working fewer hours.

This is the power of focus. By focusing on what's essential, we not only make more progress—we do so with less stress, less wasted effort, and more satisfaction. In a world that constantly pushes us to do more, essentialism is a refreshing reminder that *less is often more.*

The Problem with Overcommitment

One of the biggest obstacles to practicing essentialism is our tendency to overcommit. It's tempting to say "yes" to every opportunity that comes our way. We don't want to disappoint others, and we don't want to miss out on potential rewards. So we take on more projects, more responsibilities, and more tasks—until our schedules are bursting at the seams.

But overcommitment is a trap. The more we say "yes," the more scattered our attention becomes. We stretch ourselves too thin, and as a result, we end up doing everything poorly instead of doing a few things well. When we're overcommitted, we don't have the time or energy to focus on what really matters. Instead of making progress, we find ourselves stuck in a cycle of perpetual busyness.

Essentialism teaches us the value of saying "no." It reminds us that every time we say "yes" to something, we're also saying "no" to something else. When we agree to take on another task or project, we're often sacrificing time that could be spent on our most important goals. That's why it's crucial to be selective about where we invest our time and energy.

How to Identify What's Truly Essential

One of the most challenging aspects of essentialism is figuring out what's truly essential. With so many demands on our time, how do we know which tasks to prioritize? Fortunately, there's a simple process we can follow to determine what matters most.

1. Clarify your goal.

The first step in practicing essentialism is getting crystal clear about what you're trying to achieve. What's your most important goal? This might be a professional goal, such as growing your business or advancing your career. Or it might be a personal goal, like improving your health or spending more time with your family. Whatever it is, you need to know exactly what you're working toward. Without a clear goal, it's impossible to know what's essential.

2. Identify the high-leverage actions.

Once you've identified your goal, the next step is to figure out which actions will have the biggest impact on achieving that goal. These are your high-leverage actions—the tasks that will move the needle the most. Often, these are the tasks that require the least amount of time but produce the greatest results. For example, if your goal is to improve your health, a high-leverage action might be going for a 30-minute walk every day. It doesn't take much time, but it has a significant impact on your overall well-being.

3. Eliminate or delegate everything else.

After you've identified your high-leverage actions, it's time to eliminate or delegate the tasks that don't contribute to your goal. This can be difficult, especially if you're used to doing everything yourself. But if you want to focus on what's essential, you need to let go of the nonessential. This might mean saying "no" to new opportunities, delegating tasks to others, or simply cutting out activities that don't align with your priorities.

By following these steps, you can create a clear path to progress. Instead of being overwhelmed by a long list of tasks, you'll have a focused plan that allows you to make steady progress on your most important goals.

The 80/20 Rule: A Tool for Essentialism

A powerful tool that aligns perfectly with essentialism is the 80/20 rule, also known as the Pareto Principle. This principle states that 80% of your results come from 20% of your efforts. In other words, a small number of tasks are responsible for the majority of your success.

The key to practicing essentialism is identifying those 20% tasks and focusing on them. For example, if you're running a business, you might find that 80% of your revenue comes from 20% of your clients. If that's the case, you should focus your efforts on serving those clients better, rather than spreading yourself thin trying to please everyone.

The 80/20 rule can be applied to almost every area of life. If you're trying to improve your fitness, you might find that 80% of your results come from 20% of your workouts. Focus on the workouts that give you the most bang for your buck, and you'll see better results with less effort. The same principle applies to relationships, work projects, and personal growth. By focusing on the small number of activities that have the greatest impact, you can make significant progress without feeling overwhelmed.

Real-World Example: Steve Jobs and Apple

One of the most famous advocates of essentialism was Steve Jobs, the co-founder of Apple. When Jobs returned to Apple in 1997, the company was struggling. It had a bloated product line, producing everything from printers to digital cameras, and it was losing market share to competitors.

Jobs knew that if Apple was going to survive, it needed to focus on what it did best. So he made a bold decision: he slashed Apple's product line by 70%, cutting hundreds of products that weren't essential to the company's core mission. Instead, he focused on a small number of innovative products, such as the iMac, iPod, and iPhone.

This decision to simplify and focus paid off. By concentrating on a few key products, Apple was able to create groundbreaking innovations that revolutionized entire industries. The company went from near bankruptcy to becoming one of the most valuable companies in the world.

Jobs' approach to essentialism wasn't just about product design—it was about focus. He understood that in order to succeed, Apple needed to stop trying to do everything and start focusing on doing a few things exceptionally well. This is the essence of essentialism: focusing on what truly matters and eliminating the rest.

Action Step: Conduct an Essential Audit

Now that you understand the power of essentialism, it's time to apply it to your own life. The best way to start is by conducting an essential audit of your tasks and commitments. Here's how to do it:

01. List your current commitments.

Start by writing down everything you're currently committed to, both professionally and personally. This includes work projects, social commitments, hobbies, and even household chores.

02. Identify the high-leverage activities.

For each commitment, ask yourself: *Does this contribute to my most important goal?* If the answer is yes, keep it on your list. If the answer is no, it's time to consider whether you can eliminate or delegate it.

03. Eliminate or delegate nonessential tasks.

Once you've identified the tasks that don't align with your most important goal, take steps to eliminate or delegate them. This might involve saying "no" to future commitments, delegating tasks to others, or simply letting go of activities that don't serve your priorities.

04. Refocus on what matters.

With the nonessential tasks out of the way, you can now focus on what truly matters. By dedicating your time and energy to high-leverage activities, you'll make steady progress on your most important goals.

The Benefits of Essentialism

When you embrace essentialism, you'll experience a number of transformative benefits. First and foremost, you'll notice that your stress levels decrease. When you eliminate unnecessary tasks and commitments, you free up mental and emotional space. Instead of feeling overwhelmed by a never-ending to-do list, you'll have the clarity and focus to concentrate on what really matters.

Second, you'll find that you're more productive. This might seem counterintuitive—after all, aren't you doing less? But the truth is, when you focus on fewer things, you do them better. By dedicating your time and energy to high-leverage activities, you make more meaningful progress in less time. Instead of spinning your wheels, you'll move forward with purpose and efficiency.

Third, you'll experience a greater sense of satisfaction. When you're focused on your most important goals, every task you complete feels like a step in the right direction. You'll no longer feel like you're wasting time on trivial activities. Instead, you'll feel a deep sense of fulfillment, knowing that your efforts are aligned with your values and priorities.

Finally, essentialism leads to greater personal growth. By focusing on what truly matters, you give yourself the opportunity to develop mastery in your chosen areas. Instead of being a jack-of-all-trades and master of none, you'll become highly skilled in the areas that are most important to you. This not only leads to greater success but also deepens your sense of purpose and achievement.

Challenges of Essentialism: Why It's Hard to Say No

As powerful as essentialism is, it's not always easy to practice. One of the biggest challenges people face when trying to adopt essentialism is learning to say "no." Saying "no" to new opportunities, tasks, or requests can feel uncomfortable—especially if you're someone who enjoys helping others or fears missing out on something important.

Many of us have been conditioned to believe that saying "no" is selfish or rude. But in reality, saying "no" is one of the most powerful tools you have for protecting your time and energy. Every time you say "yes" to something nonessential, you're saying "no" to something that truly matters.

It's important to remember that saying "no" isn't about rejecting people or opportunities—it's about being selective and intentional with your time. When you say "no" to distractions, you create space for the things that align with your most important goals.

How to Say No Gracefully

If you struggle with saying "no," you're not alone. Fortunately, there are ways to do it gracefully. Here are some tips for turning down requests without damaging relationships or opportunities:

01. Be polite but firm.

You don't need to give a lengthy explanation when you say "no." A simple, polite response is often all that's needed. For example, you can say, "Thank you for thinking of me, but I'm unable to take this on right now." Being direct and clear shows respect for the other person while also honoring your own priorities.

02. Offer an alternative.

If you feel bad about turning someone down, consider offering an alternative solution. For example, you might say, "I can't take this on myself, but I can recommend someone who might be able to help." This shows that you're still willing to be helpful, even if you can't commit to the task personally.

03. Use time-based excuses.

One of the easiest ways to say "no" without causing friction is to blame it on time constraints. For example, you might say, "I'd love to help, but I don't have the bandwidth at the moment." This lets the other person know that you value their request, but you simply don't have the capacity to take it on.

04. Be honest.

In some cases, it's best to be upfront about your need to focus on your priorities. You can say something like, "I'm working on some important goals right now, so I need to be selective about where I invest my time." This sends the message that you're committed to your goals and that you take your time seriously.

Remember, saying "no" is a skill that takes practice. The more you do it, the easier it becomes. And the more you protect your time and energy, the more progress you'll make on the things that matter most.

Building a Life Around Essentialism

Practicing essentialism doesn't just apply to work or personal projects—it's a philosophy that can transform every area of your life. By focusing on what truly matters, you can design a life that's simpler, more meaningful, and more fulfilling. Here are a few ways to incorporate essentialism into different areas of your life:

01. Health and Well-Being.

Focus on the essential aspects of your health. This might mean prioritizing regular exercise, getting enough sleep, and eating nutritious foods. Instead of trying to follow every new health trend, stick to the basics that have the biggest impact on your well-being.

02. Relationships.

Essentialism can also help you cultivate deeper, more meaningful relationships. Instead of trying to maintain surface-level connections with everyone, focus on nurturing your most important relationships. Spend quality time with the people who matter most to you, and let go of relationships that drain your energy without adding value.

03. Personal Growth.

If you're constantly trying to improve in every area of life, you'll spread yourself too thin. Instead, focus on a few key areas where you want to grow and develop mastery. Whether it's learning a new skill, advancing in your career, or pursuing a personal passion, choose one or two areas to focus on at a time.

04. Work and Career.

In your professional life, essentialism can help you avoid burnout and increase your productivity. Focus on the tasks and projects that align with your career goals, and delegate or decline the rest. By doing less, you'll achieve more—and you'll enjoy greater fulfilment in your work.

Conclusion: Simplicity Leads to Success

At its core, essentialism is about simplicity. It's about stripping away the nonessential so that you can focus on what truly matters. In a world that constantly pushes us to do more, essentialism is a radical, yet effective, approach to achieving success.

By practicing essentialism, you'll not only make more progress—you'll also find that progress comes with less effort. You'll experience less stress, more clarity, and a deeper sense of fulfilment. Most importantly, you'll design a life that aligns with your values and priorities.

So, take a moment to reflect on your life. What are the nonessential tasks, commitments, and distractions that are holding you back? What would happen if you let them go? By embracing essentialism, you can create space for the things that truly matter—and that's where effortless progress begins.

05: Simplifying Decision-Making for Effortless Progress

Every day, we're faced with hundreds, if not thousands, of decisions. Some are small—like what to eat for breakfast—while others are bigger and more consequential—like whether to take on a new project or shift career paths. Each decision, no matter how small, takes up mental energy. Over time, this can lead to decision fatigue, a state in which we become mentally exhausted from making too many choices.

When decision fatigue sets in, we often make poor choices, procrastinate, or feel overwhelmed by the sheer number of options in front of us. It's one of the main reasons why people struggle to make progress, even when they know what they want to achieve.

The good news is that by simplifying your decision-making process, you can conserve mental energy, reduce stress, and make better choices. In this chapter, we'll explore how to create systems and routines that minimize the number of decisions you need to make on a daily basis. We'll also discuss strategies for making more effective decisions with less effort.

The Cost of Decision Fatigue

To understand the importance of simplifying decision-making, we need to first recognize the costs of decision fatigue. While the brain is capable of handling a vast amount of information, it has limited cognitive resources. Every decision you make, no matter how insignificant, depletes those resources. By the end of the day, after a multitude of choices, your ability to make thoughtful, deliberate decisions diminishes.

Research has shown that decision fatigue can lead to several detrimental outcomes:

- **Poor choices.** When faced with decision fatigue, people tend to choose the easiest option or avoid

making decisions altogether. This can result in poor diet choices, impulsive purchases, or neglecting important responsibilities.
- **Procrastination.** As decision fatigue sets in, the mind seeks relief. One way it does this is by putting off tasks and decisions that require focus and effort. Procrastination becomes a way to avoid further mental strain.
- **Decreased willpower.** When your brain is tired from making too many decisions, your willpower decreases. That's why sticking to a diet, a fitness routine, or any form of self-discipline becomes much harder later in the day.

Simplifying the Everyday Decisions

One of the simplest ways to combat decision fatigue is by eliminating the need to make unnecessary choices in your daily routine. This is something that high-performing individuals and thought leaders often practice. For example, Steve Jobs was known for wearing the same type of clothing every day—a black turtleneck, jeans, and sneakers. By removing the decision of what to wear each day, he preserved mental energy for more important decisions.

You don't need to go to extremes, but by simplifying daily decisions, you can create a smoother, more focused start to each day. Here are a few ways to minimize decision fatigue in your everyday life:

1. Automate routine decisions.

One of the most effective ways to simplify decision-making is by creating systems that automate routine decisions. This might mean planning your meals for the week in advance, setting a regular workout schedule, or laying out your clothes the night before. By automating these small decisions, you reduce the number of choices you have to make each day.

Another way to automate decisions is by using tools and technology. For example, setting up automatic payments for bills can relieve the burden of remembering due dates, while using productivity apps can help you manage your tasks without having to constantly prioritize or rethink your schedule.

2. Limit your options.

When you have too many options, it can feel overwhelming. Reducing the number of choices available to you simplifies the decision-making process. This is why minimalism is often connected to productivity—less clutter means fewer decisions about what to wear, what to do, or what to focus on.

Start by limiting the variety of items you use daily. This could involve simplifying your wardrobe, streamlining your workspace, or using the same tools and platforms for work consistently. For example, if you have a favorite breakfast that you know is both healthy and convenient, stick to it instead of choosing something new each morning.

3. Create routines and habits.

Routines and habits are the ultimate decision-simplifiers. Once something becomes a habit, you no longer need to consciously decide to do it—it becomes automatic. Establishing routines for your mornings, workdays, and evenings can eliminate dozens of small decisions and give you more cognitive energy for important tasks.

For instance, you might create a morning routine where you wake up at the same time, drink a glass of water, exercise for 30 minutes, and then spend time reading. These actions become automatic over time, so you don't need to deliberate each step. The more decisions you can build into routines, the more mental space you'll have for creative and complex tasks.

Decision-Making Frameworks

While simplifying everyday decisions can conserve mental energy, you still need a strategy for making more significant decisions. Simplifying decision-making for big choices is just as crucial for effortless progress. Here are some decision-making frameworks that can help you make effective choices without unnecessary complexity.

1. The Two-Minute Rule

The two-minute rule is simple: if a decision can be made or an action completed in two minutes or less, do it immediately. This rule eliminates the tendency to overthink small tasks and prevents them from piling up into overwhelming to-do lists. The more quickly you can handle small decisions, the less mental clutter you'll experience.

2. The Eisenhower Matrix

Named after President Dwight D. Eisenhower, this matrix helps you prioritize tasks by urgency and importance. It divides decisions into four categories:

- **Urgent and important:** Do these tasks immediately.
- **Important but not urgent:** Schedule these tasks for later.
- **Urgent but not important:** Delegate these tasks if possible.
- **Neither urgent nor important:** Eliminate these tasks.

This matrix not only helps you focus on what truly matters but also teaches you how to delegate or eliminate tasks that don't contribute to your long-term progress.

3. The 10/10/10 Rule

Popularized by author and businesswoman Suzy Welch, the 10/10/10 rule is a simple way to evaluate long-term consequences of a decision. Before making a choice, ask yourself:

- **How will I feel about this decision in 10 minutes?**
- **How will I feel about it in 10 months?**
- **How will I feel about it in 10 years?**

This framework helps you think beyond the present moment and consider the broader impact of your decisions. By doing so, you avoid making choices based on short-term emotions or convenience.

Reducing Mental Clutter for Better Decisions

One of the core principles of effortless progress is maintaining clarity. When your mind is cluttered with too many decisions, it's hard to focus on what really matters. To reduce mental clutter and improve decision-making, consider the following strategies:

1. Batch similar decisions.

Batching is the practice of grouping similar tasks together and handling them all at once. For example, instead of checking your email throughout the day, designate specific times to handle all your emails at once. Similarly, you can batch errands or meetings. By grouping tasks that require similar types of decisions, you reduce the number of context switches your brain has to make, which saves energy and improves focus.

2. Delegate when possible.

Learning to delegate tasks is one of the most powerful ways to free up mental energy. If someone else is capable of handling a task or decision, delegate it. This applies to both personal and professional contexts. In a work setting, delegating tasks to others can give you more time to focus on high-leverage activities. In your personal life, outsourcing tasks like grocery shopping, cleaning, or even meal prep can eliminate a range of small decisions that drain your mental energy.

3. Limit your sources of information.

We live in a world of information overload, and constantly consuming data from news, social media, and other sources can clutter your mind. Consider setting boundaries for how much information you consume each day. For example, limit your time on social media, unsubscribe from unnecessary email newsletters, and only check the news at specific times. When you streamline the information you're taking in, you have more mental space for meaningful decisions.

Decision-Making and Long-Term Progress

It's easy to think of decision-making as something that only affects the immediate moment, but the reality is that your decisions today shape your future. Whether you're choosing how to spend your time, what goals to pursue, or how to approach your work, every decision adds up.

The key to effortless progress is understanding that you don't have to make perfect decisions all the time. Instead, focus on creating systems that reduce decision fatigue and streamline your process. This allows you to make more intentional choices with less effort.

When you simplify decision-making, you free up energy to focus on what truly matters—your most important goals, your passions, and your personal growth. Over time, this leads to consistent, meaningful progress that feels natural rather than forced.

Conclusion: Making Simplicity Your Strategy

Simplifying decision-making is one of the most powerful tools for achieving effortless progress. By reducing the number of choices you make, automating routine decisions, and using decision-making frameworks, you can preserve your mental energy for the decisions that really count. The result is a life that feels more focused, intentional, and aligned with your goals.

When you make simplicity your strategy, you minimize the cognitive load that comes with daily life. This allows you to approach each day with clarity and purpose, knowing that the decisions you make—whether big or small—are contributing to your long-term progress. You're no longer bogged down by the weight of endless options or the mental exhaustion that comes from too many choices.

The key to effortless progress lies in freeing your mind from unnecessary clutter and complexity. By simplifying your decision-making, you create space for creativity, strategic thinking, and growth. As you build systems that eliminate decision fatigue, you'll find that progress comes naturally, without the constant struggle or overwhelm.

Remember, it's not about making perfect decisions at every turn. It's about building a life where the essential decisions are clear, the nonessential ones are minimized, and your path to progress is streamlined. In doing so, you'll make progress feel less like a series of exhausting choices and more like a journey where each step feels effortless.

06: Mastering Time: How to Make the Most of Every Moment

Time is one of the most valuable resources we have. No matter how successful, wealthy, or talented we are, we all have the same 24 hours in a day. Yet, some people seem to get more done, make more progress, and feel more at ease with their time than others. The secret? It's not about squeezing more activities into the day—it's about mastering time and making the most of every moment.

We often hear the phrase "time management," but managing time effectively isn't about cramming more tasks into your schedule. It's about learning how to use your time wisely, with intention and clarity. When you simplify the way you approach time, you'll find that progress becomes more natural and less stressful.

In this chapter, we'll explore how to master time by focusing on what truly matters, creating systems to optimize productivity, and avoiding common time traps that slow down your progress.

The Time Myth: Why "Busy" Isn't Productive

There's a common misconception that being busy equals being productive. People often pride themselves on having packed schedules, but more activities do not always translate to more meaningful progress. It's possible to be incredibly busy and still feel like you're not moving forward.

This is where the idea of *quality over quantity* comes into play. The goal isn't to fill your day with as many tasks as possible, but to focus on a smaller number of high-impact activities that drive you toward your goals. This requires a shift in mindset from viewing time as something to fill, to viewing it as something to optimize.

Being busy is often a form of procrastination disguised as productivity. It feels good to tick off tasks, but if those tasks aren't moving you closer to your long-term objectives, they're just distractions.

Action Step:

Take a moment to review your typical daily or weekly schedule. Are the tasks you're spending time on aligned with your biggest goals, or are they busywork? Start identifying areas where you can reduce unnecessary activities.

The Power of Time Blocking

One of the most effective techniques for mastering time is **time blocking**. This method involves dividing your day into distinct blocks of time, each dedicated to a specific task or set of tasks. Instead of multitasking and constantly shifting your focus, you dedicate uninterrupted time to each activity.

For example, if you want to dedicate time to writing a report, block off two hours in your calendar exclusively for that purpose. During this time, eliminate distractions, avoid emails, and don't allow other tasks to interfere. Time blocking works because it allows you to focus deeply on one task at a time, leading to higher-quality work and faster progress.

When implemented consistently, time blocking can turn your day into a series of productive sessions, with built-in breaks to avoid burnout.

How to Get Started with Time Blocking:

1. **Plan Your Day the Night Before.** Before going to bed, spend 5-10 minutes planning out the next day's time blocks. This helps you start your day with a clear roadmap, avoiding the morning scramble of figuring out what to focus on.
2. **Batch Similar Tasks Together.** Group similar tasks into one time block. For example, allocate one block for administrative tasks like emails and phone calls, and another block for deep, creative work like writing or brainstorming.

3. **Respect Your Blocks.** Treat your time blocks as appointments with yourself. Avoid interruptions and give each task your full attention during its allotted time.

Time blocking creates structure in your day and eliminates the mental fatigue of constantly deciding what to do next. It simplifies your time, allowing for effortless progress.

The Pomodoro Technique: A Simple Way to Stay Focused

Another effective time management strategy is the **Pomodoro Technique**. This method helps you break your work into intervals of focused effort followed by short breaks. Here's how it works:

1. **Choose a Task.** Select a task that requires your attention.
2. **Set a Timer for 25 Minutes.** Focus exclusively on the task for 25 minutes. Avoid distractions and work as efficiently as possible.
3. **Take a 5-Minute Break.** After 25 minutes of focused work, take a short break to relax and recharge.
4. **Repeat.** After completing four 25-minute intervals (known as Pomodoros), take a longer break of 15-30 minutes.

The Pomodoro Technique is effective because it creates a sense of urgency with each 25-minute session. Knowing that a break is coming motivates you to stay focused, and the frequent breaks prevent burnout.

This method works particularly well if you find it hard to stay concentrated for long periods of time. By breaking your day into smaller, manageable chunks, you reduce the mental burden and make steady progress without feeling overwhelmed.

Prioritizing the Essential: The 80/20 Rule

We've already touched on the 80/20 rule in earlier chapters, but its application in time management is critical. The 80/20 rule, or Pareto Principle, states that 80% of your results come from 20% of your efforts. In other words, a small number of tasks are responsible for the majority of your progress.

To master your time, you need to identify which 20% of activities are yielding the most significant results. This means focusing on the tasks that directly contribute to your goals and minimizing or eliminating the ones that don't.

How to Apply the 80/20 Rule to Your Time:

- **Audit Your Current Tasks.** Write down everything you do on a daily or weekly basis. Next, identify which tasks have the highest impact on your progress. These are your "20% tasks."
- **Eliminate or Delegate the Rest.** Once you've identified your most important tasks, delegate, outsource, or eliminate the remaining 80% that contribute little to your goals. This might involve saying no to certain meetings, delegating work to a colleague, or cutting down on social media use.
- **Focus on High-Impact Activities.** Spend the majority of your time on the 20% of tasks that bring the greatest rewards. These are your priority tasks, and they should take up the bulk of your time blocks.

By applying the 80/20 rule, you shift your focus from doing more to doing *better*. Your productivity will increase, and you'll make faster progress toward your goals with less effort.

Avoiding Common Time Traps

Even with the best intentions, we often fall into time traps that drain our energy and productivity. These traps can take many forms—distractions, procrastination, or overcommitting to tasks that don't align with your priorities.

Here are some of the most common time traps and how to avoid them:

1. The Multitasking Myth.

Contrary to popular belief, multitasking doesn't make you more productive. In fact, studies show that switching between tasks reduces efficiency and increases the time it takes to complete each one. The brain can only focus on one task at a time, so multitasking leads to mental fatigue and mistakes.

Solution: Focus on one task at a time, using methods like time blocking and the Pomodoro technique to stay focused. Commit to completing a task before moving on to the next one.

2. Overcommitting.

Saying "yes" to too many tasks or projects can quickly overwhelm your schedule and leave you with little time for your most important work. Overcommitting often leads to burnout and missed deadlines.

Solution: Be selective about the commitments you take on. Before saying yes to new opportunities, consider whether they align with your goals and if you have the time to dedicate to them without sacrificing quality.

3. Distractions.

In today's digital age, distractions are everywhere—social media, emails, notifications, and even colleagues. These interruptions break your focus and significantly reduce your productivity.

Solution: Create boundaries for yourself when it comes to distractions. Silence notifications during work periods, set specific times to check email, and consider using productivity apps that block distracting websites during focus time.

By recognizing and avoiding these common time traps, you'll free up more time and energy to focus on tasks that truly matter.

The Role of Energy in Time Management

While time is a fixed resource, energy fluctuates throughout the day. The ability to master time isn't just about fitting tasks into your schedule—it's about aligning those tasks with your energy levels. Energy management is a critical, yet often overlooked, component of time mastery.

Understanding Your Energy Peaks and Valleys:

Each person has periods of high energy and low energy throughout the day. For example, many people feel most alert and productive in the morning, while their energy dips in the early afternoon. Others may experience a burst of creative energy in the evening. The key to effective time management is to align your most important tasks with your natural energy peaks.

Action Step: Map Out Your Energy Levels:

For one week, track your energy levels throughout the day. Note when you feel most energized and when you experience dips in focus or motivation. Once you identify your energy patterns, schedule your high-priority tasks during peak energy periods and save lower-priority tasks for times when your energy is lower.

Rest and Recharge:

Time management is not just about working efficiently—it's also about knowing when to rest. Just as you block time for work, block time for rest and relaxation. Taking breaks throughout the day allows your brain to recharge, making you more productive when you return to work.

Case Studies: Time Mastery in Action

To better understand how mastering time can lead to effortless progress, let's look at some real-life examples of individuals who have excelled by simplifying their approach to time management.

1. Elon Musk: The Power of Structured Schedules

Elon Musk, known for running multiple companies, including Tesla and SpaceX, attributes much of his productivity to a technique called **time blocking**. Musk plans his day in five-minute increments, ensuring that every moment is accounted for and that his time is used efficiently. This method prevents time from slipping away in unproductive activities.

While Musk's schedule is intense, it demonstrates the power of structure in time management. By being intentional about how you allocate your time, you can make significant progress in multiple areas of life.

2. Serena Williams: Prioritizing Rest and Focus

Tennis champion Serena Williams has been vocal about the importance of rest in maintaining peak performance. While she spends hours training, she also prioritizes sleep, meditation, and recovery. Williams understands that mastering time isn't about being constantly busy—it's about balancing effort with rest to ensure sustainable progress.

Williams also uses focus techniques, like visualizing success before matches, to align her mental energy with her physical training. Her approach to time management allows her to maintain focus during high-stakes moments while preventing burnout.

Creating a Daily Rhythm for Effortless Time Management

To truly master your time, it's essential to create a daily rhythm that supports productivity and progress. This rhythm doesn't have to be rigid; in fact, it should be flexible enough to adapt to changes but structured enough to provide a framework for getting things done.

Start Your Day with Intent.

The first hour of your day sets the tone for the rest of it. Begin each day with a clear intention. This could be a written list of your top three priorities, a mental review of your goals, or simply a few moments of mindfulness to set a positive mindset.

End Your Day with Reflection.

At the end of each day, take a few minutes to reflect on what you accomplished. What worked well? What didn't? By regularly reviewing your progress, you'll gain insights into how to optimize your time even further.

Build in Breaks and Downtime.

Remember that managing time effectively isn't about working non-stop. Build in breaks throughout your day to recharge, and don't forget to allocate downtime for activities that bring you joy and relaxation. Rest is essential for sustained productivity.

Conclusion: Time as an Ally, Not an Enemy

Mastering time doesn't mean controlling every minute of your day—it means learning how to make time work for you, not against you. When you focus on the right tasks, eliminate distractions, and create a rhythm that supports your goals, you turn time into an ally rather than an enemy.

By simplifying your approach to time management—whether through time blocking, the Pomodoro technique, or prioritizing high-impact activities—you'll find that progress becomes more natural. It's no longer a race against the clock, but a steady, purposeful journey toward your goals.

Remember, the key isn't to work harder or longer but to work smarter. Use your time intentionally, stay focused on what truly matters, and allow yourself the flexibility to rest and recharge. When you manage your time in alignment with your priorities, you create a sense of ease and flow in your day-to-day life.

Mastering time is not about perfection—it's about consistency. It's about showing up each day with a plan, adjusting when needed, and moving forward with clarity. As you continue to refine your time management strategies, you'll find that your productivity increases, your stress decreases, and your progress feels effortless.

Ultimately, time is one of your greatest resources. When you learn to master it, you'll unlock a new level of efficiency and effectiveness, allowing you to make the most of every moment.

07: Navigating Common Obstacles on the Path to Effortless Progress

Every journey comes with its challenges, and the path to effortless progress is no exception. Even with the best systems, habits, and routines in place, obstacles can arise. The key isn't to avoid these challenges entirely—it's learning how to navigate them effectively. This chapter explores common obstacles that may stand in the way of your progress and offers practical solutions grounded in research and proven strategies.

Section 1: Time Management Challenges

Obstacle: Feeling like there's never enough time to focus on systems and routines.

For many people, the idea of adopting new systems or routines feels overwhelming simply because they believe they don't have enough time. The pressure of daily life, including work commitments, family responsibilities, and personal goals, can make it feel as though there is no room for improvement, no space for building habits that last. This scarcity of time becomes a significant mental barrier.

However, research shows that this feeling often stems not from a lack of time, but from the way time is managed. A study from **Harvard Business School** found that people who schedule and prioritize their most important tasks at the start of the day tend to experience greater productivity and less stress compared to those who allow their schedules to fill up reactively .

The real challenge isn't time—it's how we manage it.

Solution: *Time audits, micro-systems, and prioritization techniques.*

One of the most effective ways to overcome time management challenges is to conduct a **time audit**. A study published in *The Journal of Organizational Behavior* found that employees who regularly assessed their time and tasks experienced less stress and greater productivity compared to those who didn't prioritize their time management techniques .

Conduct a time audit by tracking your activities for a week to identify where your time is being spent. This exercise often reveals "hidden" pockets of time that can be used more effectively. Once you identify where your time goes, you can eliminate nonessential tasks or delegate them.

For example, take the case of **Martha**, a project manager who constantly felt overwhelmed by meetings. After conducting a time audit, she realized that many of the meetings were unnecessary, could be shortened, or could be replaced with quick check-ins. By eliminating 30% of her weekly meetings, Martha gained several hours of focused work time that she used to improve her productivity and build new systems.

Next, implement **micro-systems**. Instead of attempting to overhaul your entire schedule, start by creating small, manageable routines that fit within your current time constraints. Research shows that starting small and scaling up as you experience success leads to higher long-term adherence to routines .

Micro-systems are bite-sized versions of larger routines that fit into even the busiest of days. For example, instead of blocking an hour for exercise, you can start with 10-minute micro-workouts that fit into your schedule. Over time, these micro-systems compound into larger routines, and they feel manageable because you've built them incrementally.

Lastly, apply **the 80/20 rule** (also known as the Pareto Principle). This rule suggests that 80% of results come from 20% of your efforts. Identify the 20% of tasks or systems that have the greatest impact on your progress and focus on those. By prioritizing high-impact tasks, you'll see more results without needing to spend extra time.

Additional Strategy: Time Blocking and Boundaries

Time blocking is a powerful method to ensure that your most important tasks get done. Research published in the *Harvard Business Review* showed that workers who time-blocked at least two hours of uninterrupted, deep work each day reported a 25% increase in productivity and greater job satisfaction compared to those who didn't .

To make time blocking effective, establish clear **boundaries** during your work blocks. Notify colleagues or family members that you're unavailable during these periods and reduce distractions by turning off notifications, silencing your phone, and using tools like website blockers to keep your focus intact.

Real-Life Example: Consider the case of **Jake**, a software engineer who found himself constantly interrupted by notifications and colleagues asking for help. By implementing time-blocked "focus hours" and informing his team about these blocks, he was able to reclaim his productivity and complete his most complex tasks without distraction. Over time, his work quality improved, and he even finished projects ahead of schedule.

Section 2: Decision Fatigue and Overwhelm

Obstacle: Too many decisions leading to paralysis or feeling overwhelmed.

Decision fatigue occurs when the brain becomes exhausted from making too many choices, leading to poorer decision-making and procrastination. **Roy Baumeister**'s research on decision fatigue found that as people make more decisions throughout the day, their ability to make high-quality decisions deteriorates, leading to impulse decisions or avoidance .

This is particularly relevant for those trying to simplify their lives but finding themselves overwhelmed by too many choices. Whether it's choosing the right system to implement or deciding how to prioritize goals, decision fatigue can slow or stall progress entirely.

Solution: *Automate small decisions and batch decision-making.*

To combat decision fatigue, start by **automating small, repetitive decisions**. This strategy works because it removes the need for constant decision-making on trivial matters, freeing up cognitive resources for more important tasks. A simple example is creating a **capsule wardrobe** where all of your clothing items are versatile and match each other. This eliminates the need to spend time each morning deciding what to wear.

Successful leaders like **Mark Zuckerberg** and **Barack Obama** famously simplified their wardrobes to avoid decision fatigue, allowing them to focus their cognitive energy on more critical tasks. This aligns with findings from a study in *The Journal of Personality and Social Psychology*, which suggests that reducing unnecessary choices helps conserve mental resources for more critical decisions .

Another effective technique is **batch decision-making**, where you consolidate decision-making tasks into set blocks of time. For instance, instead of deciding what to eat for dinner every night, you can plan and prepare your meals for the week on Sunday. This eliminates daily decision-making and saves time and mental energy.

Real-Life Example: Emma, a busy entrepreneur, used to spend the first hour of her workday deciding what tasks to prioritize. This daily indecision delayed her productivity and created unnecessary stress. By batching her decision-making on Sunday evenings, Emma began planning her week in advance and aligning her tasks with her larger goals. She found that by starting each day with a clear plan, her focus improved, and she completed tasks more efficiently.

Section 3: Motivation Dips

Obstacle: Inconsistent motivation leading to failure in maintaining habits.

Motivation is often high when starting a new routine or system, but over time, it can dip. This can lead to a drop-off in consistency and, ultimately, failure to sustain progress. A study published in The European Journal of Social Psychology found that building automatic behaviors (habits) takes, on average, 66 days. However, motivation tends to waver during this period, which is why many people give up .

The problem with relying on motivation alone is that it fluctuates based on emotions, energy levels, and external factors. What happens when motivation fades? That's where systems come into play.

Solution: Rely on systems and external accountability.

Rather than relying solely on motivation, focus on creating **systems that make action automatic**. This means integrating your habits into your daily routine in such a way that they don't require a conscious decision. As habits become automatic, they rely less on fluctuating motivation levels. For instance, if your goal is to exercise regularly, scheduling your workout at the same time every day makes it part of your routine rather than a decision you need to make daily.

A study by **Lally et al. (2010)** showed that consistent repetition of actions at the same time each day is one of the most effective ways to build automatic habits. By creating a stable routine, you reduce the dependency on motivation and increase the likelihood of sticking with the habit long-term.

To support this, build in **external accountability**. A study from the American Society of Training and Development found that people are 65% more likely to meet their goals when they commit to someone else, and this likelihood increases to 95% when they have regular accountability meetings . This could be as simple as finding an accountability partner or joining a group focused on the same goals.

Additionally, using **small rewards** to celebrate progress can help maintain motivation during dips. These rewards don't have to be extravagant—they can be as simple as allowing yourself extra leisure time after completing a key task or enjoying a favorite activity after staying consistent for a week.

Case Study: Tom, a freelance graphic designer, struggled with keeping up a consistent schedule for working out. His motivation fluctuated based on how busy he was with client projects. To address this, Tom implemented a system where he worked out every morning before checking his emails. By turning the action into a routine that occurred at the same time daily, he no longer relied on motivation to get moving. He also joined an online accountability group, which kept him motivated to stay on track by sharing his weekly progress.

Section 4: Setbacks and Perfectionism

Obstacle: Setbacks or missed goals leading to feelings of failure or the need for perfection.

Setbacks are inevitable, and many people struggle with the mental blocks that follow them. For those with perfectionist tendencies, missing a goal or breaking a habit can lead to feelings of failure or a sense that all progress has been lost. This often results in an "all-or-nothing" mindset, where one mistake is seen as complete failure.

Research conducted by **Dr. Carol Dweck**, a psychologist at Stanford University, highlights the difference between a **fixed mindset** and a **growth mindset**. People with a fixed mindset believe their abilities are static, which causes them to fear failure. In contrast, those with a growth mindset see failures as opportunities to learn and improve. Dweck's work has shown that individuals with a growth mindset are more resilient, more likely to embrace challenges, and less likely to give up after setbacks .

Solution: Reframe setbacks and embrace progress over perfection.

The concept of **"failing forward"** is essential for overcoming setbacks. Instead of viewing failure as the end of the road, see it as a learning opportunity. Research on the **growth mindset** by psychologist Carol Dweck demonstrates that individuals who believe in their ability to grow from challenges are far more likely to persevere and achieve success .

When facing setbacks, try to reframe them as feedback rather than failure. Ask yourself: What can I learn from this? How can I adjust my systems to prevent this in the future?

Additionally, embrace the principle of **progress over perfection**. Perfectionism often leads to paralysis, where fear of making a mistake prevents action altogether. Instead, focus on small, incremental progress. If you miss a day of your habit, simply get back on track the next day without overthinking it.

Real-Life Example: Lucy, an aspiring writer, set a goal of writing 1,000 words per day for her novel. She managed to maintain this routine for a few weeks but eventually missed a day due to other commitments. Instead of viewing it as a failure, Lucy used the growth mindset approach to reassess her goals. She lowered her daily word count to 500 but committed to consistency. By accepting small progress, Lucy finished her novel over time without feeling the pressure of perfectionism.

Section 5: Information Overload

Obstacle: Consuming too much information and feeling unsure about the right direction.

In the digital age, access to information is at an all-time high. While this can be beneficial, it can also lead to **information overload**, a state in which an individual becomes overwhelmed by too much data and finds it difficult to make decisions or take action. A study by **Iyengar and Lepper** on choice overload showed that when presented with too many options, individuals were less likely to make a decision and more likely to experience regret after making one .

Solution: Limit information intake and curate your learning resources.

To combat information overload, set clear **learning goals** and define what you need to know to take action. Curate your information sources by identifying high-quality resources and limiting the number of channels you rely on.

In a world overflowing with information, it's important to learn how to **filter** and **prioritize** information that aligns with your goals. One way to do this is by practicing **just-in-time learning**—only seeking out information when it's immediately applicable to a current goal or task. This prevents the accumulation of irrelevant data and keeps your focus sharp.

Another solution is to create a **learning curation system**. This involves subscribing only to trusted, high-quality information sources—whether they be books, blogs, or podcasts—and limiting your exposure to unnecessary content.

Case Study: David, an aspiring entrepreneur, used to spend hours each week consuming business podcasts, blogs, and online courses. While this was valuable in the beginning, he found himself overwhelmed by the sheer volume of advice and conflicting opinions. To combat this, David created a curated list of four key resources that aligned with his specific business goals. He limited his information intake to these resources, which significantly reduced his feelings of overwhelm and allowed him to take more focused action.

Conclusion

Progress isn't about avoiding obstacles—it's about learning how to navigate them effectively. Whether it's time constraints, decision fatigue, motivation dips, setbacks, or information overload, challenges are a natural part of the journey toward effortless progress. With the right strategies in place, you can overcome these barriers and continue moving forward.

Remember, progress is not a straight line. It's okay to face setbacks, lose motivation, or feel overwhelmed at times. What matters most is your ability to bounce back, adjust your systems, and stay consistent. By adopting these solutions and staying committed to your goals, you'll find that even the most challenging obstacles can be overcome on the path to effortless progress.

08: The Power of Systems: Creating Structures that Lead to Progress

Progress doesn't happen by chance. It happens through consistent effort, guided by effective systems. While motivation and willpower play a role in helping us get started, they are often unreliable over the long term. Life's distractions, challenges, and shifting priorities can easily derail our progress if we don't have structures in place to keep us moving forward.

Systems are the key to simplifying your journey toward success. Instead of relying on sheer discipline to complete tasks or achieve goals, you create frameworks that make progress automatic. Systems turn your daily habits and routines into a well-oiled machine that works for you, even on days when you lack motivation.

In this chapter, we'll explore how to design systems that support your long-term goals, simplify your routines, and create effortless progress. With the right systems in place, achieving what once seemed difficult will become part of your daily life.

Why Systems Matter More than Goals

Many people set goals—lose 20 pounds, write a book, get promoted—but they often fall short because they focus too much on the outcome and not enough on the process. While goals provide direction, systems are the mechanism that get you there.

Goals are about the destination, but systems are about the journey. They dictate the actions you take on a daily basis to move you closer to your goals. Consider the example of an athlete. While the goal may be to win a championship, it's the system of daily practice, conditioning, and nutrition that makes winning possible. The goal is the outcome, but the system is what leads to success.

Here's why systems matter more than goals:

- **Consistency Over Intensity:** Goals often encourage short bursts of intense effort, but systems promote long-term consistency. Instead of cramming to meet a deadline or sprinting through a project, a system provides a steady pace of progress.
- **Process-Oriented:** When you focus on systems, you're thinking about the process, not just the result. This keeps you engaged, even when the goal seems far off. It also makes the journey more rewarding because you're making progress every day.
- **Resilience Against Failure:** Goals are binary—you either achieve them, or you don't. Systems, however, focus on continuous improvement. Even if you face setbacks, a strong system helps you get back on track quickly, without feeling like a failure.
- **Removes Decision Fatigue:** Systems help you automate decisions. Instead of having to choose what to do next or whether to take action, your system determines your next steps. This reduces decision fatigue and ensures you stay on course.

How to Build Effective Systems for Progress

The key to effortless progress is building systems that work for you, not against you. A system can be as simple as a morning routine or as complex as a project management process. The goal is to create a structure that simplifies decision-making and keeps you moving forward consistently.

Here's how to start building effective systems:

1. Identify Your Goals and Priorities

Before you can build a system, you need to know what you're trying to achieve. What are your long-term goals? What are the most important areas of your life where you want to make progress? These could be related to your career, health, relationships, or personal growth.

Once you have your goals, break them down into smaller, actionable steps. These steps form the foundation of your system. For example, if your goal is to write a book, your system might include writing 500 words every morning, rather than focusing on the entire book as a daunting task.

2. Simplify Your Actions

One of the most important principles of building systems is simplicity. The more complicated your system, the harder it is to maintain. Keep your actions simple and straightforward, so they become easy to follow, even on busy or low-energy days.

For example, if your goal is to get in shape, don't create a complex workout routine that requires special equipment and extensive planning. Instead, start with a system as simple as doing bodyweight exercises at home for 15 minutes each day. Once you're consistent with that, you can expand and adjust as needed.

The simpler your system, the more likely you are to stick with it.

3. Create Habits, Not Just Tasks

Systems are most effective when they are built around habits, not just one-off tasks. A habit is something you do regularly without needing to think about it, while tasks require conscious effort and decision-making.

For example, if you want to improve your productivity at work, create a habit of starting your day by reviewing your to-do list and prioritizing tasks. This simple habit sets the tone for the entire day and becomes automatic over time.

To turn tasks into habits:

- **Start small.** Begin with something you can do in five minutes or less. Once that becomes part of your routine, you can build on it.

- **Use triggers.** Create a trigger that reminds you to perform the habit. For example, if you want to start journaling, make it a habit to do so right after your morning coffee.
- **Repetition is key.** The more you repeat an action, the more ingrained it becomes in your routine. Over time, it will feel effortless.

Examples of Systems for Everyday Life

Now that we've covered the basics of building systems, let's look at some practical examples of systems you can implement in different areas of your life to achieve effortless progress.

1. A System for Health and Fitness

Goal: Get fit and stay healthy. System: Create a daily workout habit that fits into your schedule, combined with a meal-planning system.

Morning Routine: Set aside 15-30 minutes for exercise every morning. Keep it simple with bodyweight exercises, yoga, or a quick run. By doing it first thing in the morning, you eliminate the possibility of other tasks getting in the way later in the day.

Meal Planning: Prepare your meals for the week every Sunday. Plan healthy, balanced meals, and prep ingredients in advance to reduce the temptation to eat unhealthy foods when you're busy.

By having a workout and meal-planning system, you take the guesswork out of health decisions and automate the steps needed for maintaining fitness.

2. A System for Personal Development

Goal: Read more books and expand your knowledge. System: Implement a reading system that makes learning part of your daily routine.

Daily Reading Habit: Set aside 20-30 minutes every day to read. Whether it's in the morning, during lunch, or before bed, make reading a consistent part of your day. Instead of aiming to finish a book in a week, focus on reading just a few pages every day.

Tracking Progress: Keep a simple journal or app where you log your daily reading progress. This reinforces the habit and helps you see how much you've read over time.

A reading system makes personal growth an automatic part of your life. Over time, you'll be amazed at how much you've learned without feeling like you had to find extra time.

3. A System for Professional Growth

Goal: Advance in your career or business. System: Build a system for professional development that includes setting priorities, tracking tasks, and learning new skills.

Task Prioritization: Start each day by reviewing your key objectives for the week. Use a system like time blocking to allocate specific times for deep work, meetings, and professional learning.

Skill Development: Set aside one day each week to focus on learning a new skill that advances your career. This could include online courses, books, or mentorship sessions.

Networking: Make a habit of reaching out to one new person in your industry each week, whether it's via LinkedIn, email, or at a networking event. Building connections should be part of your professional system, not an afterthought.

With a career system in place, you can make progress toward your professional goals without feeling overwhelmed by the day-to-day demands of your job.

Automating Your Systems for Maximum Efficiency

The ultimate goal of creating systems is to make progress feel effortless. One way to achieve this is by automating parts of your system so they require even less thought or effort. Automation can help you streamline processes and free up mental energy for more creative and strategic tasks.

Here's how to automate your systems:

1. Use Technology

Technology is a powerful tool for system automation. From task management apps to automatic reminders, technology can take care of repetitive tasks and ensure you stay on track. Here are some examples:

- **Project Management Tools:** Apps like Trello, Asana, or Notion can help you keep track of your tasks, set deadlines, and automate recurring tasks. You can set up templates for routine processes, making it easier to manage projects.
- **Habit Tracking Apps:** Apps like Habitica or Streaks can help you track your habits and provide reminders to keep you consistent.
- **Time Tracking:** Use time tracking apps to monitor how much time you're spending on different activities. This can help you identify where you're most productive and where you may need to adjust your system.

2. Set Up Recurring Actions

Automate recurring tasks to save time and mental energy. For example:

Automate Bill Payments: Set up automatic payments for your utilities, rent, and other recurring bills. This eliminates the need to remember due dates and reduces financial stress.

Schedule Regular Tasks: Use your calendar to schedule regular tasks, like cleaning, meal prepping, or exercise. Once scheduled, you don't have to think about when to do them—they become part of your system.

3. Delegate to Others

Automation isn't limited to technology. Delegating tasks to others is another form of system automation. If you can afford to outsource tasks that aren't essential for you to personally handle, such as administrative work, cleaning, or even errands, you free up time for activities that align with your strengths and priorities.

When you delegate, you effectively multiply your efforts. The tasks still get done, but you're not the one responsible for them. This is especially helpful for professionals and entrepreneurs who need to focus on high-level activities such as strategy, growth, and leadership.

Consider the areas of your life where you can outsource tasks or responsibilities. It might be as simple as hiring a virtual assistant to handle routine emails or asking a family member to take on certain household chores. Remember, delegating isn't about avoiding responsibility—it's about prioritizing your time and ensuring that every action aligns with your larger goals.

Feedback Loops: Improving Your Systems Over Time

One of the most valuable aspects of systems is their ability to evolve and improve. A system isn't something you set once and forget—it's a structure that should be regularly reviewed and optimized. This is where *feedback loops* come in.

A feedback loop is the process of assessing the effectiveness of your system, identifying areas for improvement, and making adjustments. It ensures that your system continues to serve your goals and adapts to changing circumstances.

1. Regular Reviews

Set aside time at regular intervals to review your systems. This could be a weekly, monthly, or quarterly check-in, depending on the system's complexity. During these reviews, ask yourself:

- Is the system still helping me progress toward my goals?
- Are there any bottlenecks or inefficiencies that need to be addressed?
- Are there any new tools or methods I could implement to improve the system?

By regularly reviewing your system, you ensure that it stays relevant and effective. You'll also notice when a system becomes outdated or when you've reached a stage where certain parts of the system can be eliminated or simplified further.

2. Measure Your Progress

For a system to be truly effective, it needs to have measurable outcomes. For example, if you've set up a system for writing a book, track how many words you've written each week or how many chapters you've completed. If you have a fitness system, measure your progress by tracking workout consistency or improvements in your strength and endurance.

Measuring progress not only keeps you motivated but also provides concrete evidence of your efforts. It's easier to refine your system when you can see what's working and what needs adjustment.

3. Adapt to Change

Life is dynamic, and your systems should be, too. If you experience significant changes—whether personal, professional, or circumstantial—don't be afraid to adjust your systems. For instance, if you've recently changed jobs, moved, or started a family, you may need to tweak your systems to fit your new reality.

The goal is to create systems that are resilient and flexible enough to evolve with you. The best systems are those that can adapt while still maintaining a structure that supports your progress.

The Mindset Shift: Trusting the System

One of the most important components of system-building is trusting the process. Many people feel a temptation to micromanage every detail of their lives, which leads to burnout and frustration. Systems allow you to step back and let the process work for you, rather than you constantly working to manage the process.

Trusting the system means believing in the structure you've created, even on days when you don't see immediate results. Just like an athlete who trusts their training regimen, or a business leader who trusts their team, trusting your system helps you maintain consistency and avoid overthinking or second-guessing your actions.

Letting Go of Perfection:

Trusting the system also means letting go of the need for perfection. Systems are about progress, not perfection. There will be days when things don't go as planned, or when you feel like you're not making headway. But if your system is strong, those moments won't derail you. Instead of focusing on individual failures, you can trust that the system will get you back on track.

Celebrate Small Wins:

Part of trusting the system is recognizing and celebrating small wins. Every time you complete a part of your system—whether it's sticking to your exercise routine, completing a weekly project, or even just maintaining a daily habit—it's a win. These small victories reinforce the effectiveness of your system and build momentum for bigger successes.

Case Study: Systems in Action

To illustrate the power of systems, let's explore the real-life example of a company that used systems to achieve incredible success: **Amazon**. Under the leadership of Jeff Bezos, Amazon built one of the most efficient and scalable systems in the world, transforming from a simple online bookstore into a global marketplace that revolutionized e-commerce.

Amazon's success can be largely attributed to its relentless focus on systems. From its sophisticated logistics network to its data-driven algorithms, every part of Amazon's operation is built on systems that automate processes, improve efficiency, and scale effortlessly.

For example, Amazon's recommendation algorithm is a system that automatically suggests products based on customer behavior. It works in the background, constantly learning and improving, without requiring manual intervention. This system drives billions of dollars in sales, all while operating seamlessly.

Amazon's operational systems—such as its warehouse automation, fulfillment processes, and supply chain management—allow the company to handle massive volumes of orders with speed and precision. These systems enable Amazon to deliver products quickly and cost-effectively, which has become a cornerstone of its business model.

While Amazon's systems are complex, the principle behind them is simple: create structures that run efficiently and scale without requiring constant attention. This same approach can be applied to individual goals, whether you're running a business or building personal habits.

Building Systems for Long-Term Success

The beauty of systems is that they create a foundation for long-term success. Unlike short-term bursts of motivation, systems provide stability and continuity. They allow you to make steady progress even when life gets busy or when your motivation wanes.

The Long Game:

Think of systems as playing the long game. You're not chasing immediate results or quick fixes; instead, you're building sustainable habits and processes that will carry you through the ups and downs of life. With systems, you can keep moving forward, one step at a time, without feeling overwhelmed or burnt out.

Systems Compound Over Time:

One of the most powerful aspects of systems is that they compound over time. Just like compound interest in finance, the small actions you take every day through your systems add up to significant results over the months and years. Whether it's learning a new skill, saving money, improving your fitness, or building a business, systems help you achieve exponential growth by creating consistency.

Systems are Personal:

Your systems should be personalized to fit your life, goals, and preferences. What works for someone else might not work for you—and that's okay. The key is to design systems that align with your unique strengths, lifestyle, and long-term vision. As you experiment and refine, you'll discover what systems resonate with you and what drives your progress most effectively.

Conclusion: Make Systems Your Strategy for Effortless Progress

The most successful people aren't necessarily those with the greatest talent or the most motivation—they're the ones who have built systems that allow them to make consistent progress over time. Systems turn chaos into clarity, uncertainty into structure, and fleeting motivation into sustained action.

The beauty of systems is that they free you from the pressure of constantly thinking about what to do next or worrying about slipping off track. With a well-designed system in place, progress becomes a natural byproduct of your daily life. Instead of struggling to stay disciplined, you create an environment that makes success inevitable.

As you move forward in your journey toward effortless progress, remember that the true power of systems lies in their simplicity and consistency. Start small, experiment, and refine your systems over time. Trust the process, celebrate the small wins, and watch as your systems compound into significant achievements.

In the end, systems are not just about reaching your goals—they're about transforming the way you live and work. When you make systems your strategy, you'll find that progress becomes less about effort and more about flow.

09: Sustaining Effortless Progress: Building a Life of Simplicity and Achievement

By now, you've explored the power of simplifying your life—streamlining decision-making, mastering your time, and building systems that support long-term progress. As you've journeyed through this book, the recurring theme has been clear: success doesn't have to be complicated. It's not about working harder, juggling more tasks, or achieving fleeting wins. It's about creating a life where progress feels natural, sustainable, and aligned with your values.

In this final chapter, we'll explore how you can sustain the momentum you've built. Sustaining effortless progress is about making your systems, habits, and routines work for you in the long run. It's about continuing to refine, simplify, and adjust your approach as you grow. The goal isn't perfection but steady improvement—a life where simplicity and achievement coexist harmoniously.

The Mindset of Sustainable Progress

Progress is not linear—it's a process of continuous learning, adapting, and growth. While the systems, habits, and strategies you've put into place will help you make steady progress, maintaining that progress requires a mindset of resilience and adaptability.

1. Progress Is a Journey, Not a Destination

In the journey toward sustained success, it's important to remember that progress is ongoing. There is no final destination where you'll have accomplished everything you need to achieve. Instead, progress is a series of steps, each leading you to new opportunities for growth.

The idea of progress as a journey is crucial because it shifts your focus from being obsessed with an end goal to appreciating the process itself. When you learn to enjoy the steps along the way, you'll find that setbacks don't feel as frustrating and successes feel more rewarding.

One example of this mindset shift can be found in the way marathon runners approach their training. While crossing the finish line may be the ultimate goal, they derive a sense of accomplishment from each day of practice, each increase in endurance, and each new personal best. The journey becomes the reward.

- **Action Step**: Reflect on an area of your life where you've been fixated on the destination. What can you do to enjoy the process more? How can you celebrate the small wins along the way?

2. Embrace Adaptability

Adaptability is one of the most important traits for sustaining progress. Life is unpredictable, and your ability to adjust and respond to new challenges will determine whether you can maintain your momentum.

Adaptability also means being open to change and growth. The strategies and systems that work today may not work tomorrow, and that's okay. What's important is your willingness to experiment, refine, and iterate on your systems and habits to fit your evolving life circumstances.

- **Case Study**: Consider the example of **Netflix**, a company that began as a DVD rental service but adapted to the rise of streaming. By shifting their business model and embracing new technology, they sustained growth even as the industry changed. Their adaptability allowed them to thrive while many other DVD rental companies fell behind.

In your personal life, this same principle applies. Whether you're adjusting your workout routine, switching careers, or shifting priorities to accommodate family changes, adaptability ensures that you stay on track despite external forces.

3. Dealing with Setbacks

Setbacks are inevitable on any long-term journey, but they don't have to derail your progress. When faced with setbacks, whether it's a missed workout, a failed project, or a personal challenge, it's important to maintain perspective.

Rather than viewing setbacks as failures, see them as opportunities for growth and learning. Every setback provides valuable feedback on what's working and what isn't. Instead of being discouraged, use setbacks to refine your systems and continue moving forward.

- **Mindset Shift**: Instead of asking, "Why did I fail?" ask, "What can I learn from this?" This subtle shift in mindset turns every setback into a stepping stone for future success.

4. The Growth vs. Comfort Zone Dichotomy

Sustained progress requires the ability to navigate the balance between comfort and growth. While it's important to build systems and habits that make progress easier, you also need to challenge yourself regularly to step out of your comfort zone. Growth happens when you're pushing your limits and expanding your capabilities.

- **Example**: Professional athletes, for instance, understand the importance of training just beyond their comfort zone. They know that real improvement happens when they challenge themselves to lift a little heavier, run a little faster, or train a little longer than before.

Stepping out of your comfort zone doesn't mean overwhelming yourself with massive challenges. Instead, it means regularly seeking out opportunities for incremental growth. Whether it's taking on a new project at work, learning a new skill, or tackling a personal challenge, these small steps outside your comfort zone compound over time into significant progress.

Key Strategies for Sustaining Effortless Progress

Sustaining progress is about creating a lifestyle that naturally supports growth. The following strategies are designed to help you maintain your momentum while keeping things simple and focused.

1. Continue Simplifying

The simpler your systems, goals, and routines, the easier they are to maintain. As life becomes more complex, simplicity helps you stay grounded. Here are some additional ways to simplify every aspect of your life.

- **Simplify Decision-Making:** Use the strategies from previous chapters to continue reducing decision fatigue. This could mean setting "default decisions" for common choices (such as always eating a particular healthy meal on Mondays) or using templates and checklists for recurring tasks.
- **Simplify Financial Systems:** Automating your finances is one of the easiest ways to reduce complexity. Set up automated savings, investments, and bill payments to ensure your financial life runs smoothly without constant intervention. This allows you to focus your energy on more important areas of your life.
- **Simplify Social Commitments:** In today's busy world, social obligations can easily become overwhelming. To prevent burnout, be selective about the social events you attend. Learn to say no when commitments don't align with your goals or values. This gives you the freedom to focus on relationships that bring meaning to your life.

2. Develop a Weekly Review Practice

One of the most powerful strategies for maintaining effortless progress is the weekly review. This is a simple practice where you reflect on the past week, assess what worked and what didn't, and plan for the week ahead.

- **Set aside time each week** to review your goals, systems, and habits. During this review, ask yourself:
    - What progress did I make toward my goals this week?
    - What obstacles did I face, and how can I overcome them moving forward?
    - Are my current systems still working effectively, or do I need to adjust them?

A weekly review helps you stay intentional about your progress and keeps you focused on what matters most.

The Power of Long-Term Habits

Habits are the backbone of long-term success, and in this section, we'll dive deeper into how to strengthen and sustain the habits you've built. Habits are what turn daily actions into automatic behaviors, removing friction from your progress.

1. Building Keystone Habits

Keystone habits are powerful because they act as triggers for other positive behaviors. When you establish a keystone habit, it sets off a chain reaction that leads to improvements in other areas of your life.

- **Example:** For many people, regular exercise is a keystone habit. Not only does it improve physical fitness, but it also leads to better sleep, improved mental clarity, and healthier eating habits.
- **Identify Your Keystone Habits:** What habits can you build that will have a cascading effect on other areas of your life? Is it a morning meditation practice that helps you stay focused throughout the day? Or perhaps it's a

habit of reviewing your goals each week, which keeps you aligned and on track.

2. Habit Stacking

One of the easiest ways to build new habits is through habit stacking, a concept popularized by James Clear in his book *Atomic Habits*. Habit stacking involves linking a new habit to an existing one, making it easier to adopt without much additional effort.

- **How to Use Habit Stacking:** If you already have a habit of brushing your teeth each morning, stack a new habit on top of it. For example, after brushing your teeth, you could meditate for 5 minutes. Because you already have the routine of brushing your teeth, the new habit of meditating becomes easier to stick with.

Habit stacking is a simple but powerful way to build long-term habits without overwhelming yourself.

3. Dealing with Habit Breaks

No matter how strong your habits are, there will inevitably be times when you break them. Whether it's due to travel, illness, or a busy schedule, habit breaks happen. The key is not to let a single break turn into a permanent lapse.

- **Action Step:** When you break a habit, don't dwell on it. Instead, focus on restarting as quickly as possible. One missed day isn't a problem, but multiple missed days can lead to the loss of the habit. The quicker you get back on track, the less damage is done.

Creating Balance and Preventing Burnout

Sustaining progress requires balance—without it, even the best systems and habits can lead to burnout. Here are strategies for maintaining balance and preventing burnout over the long term.

1. Integrating Play and Creativity

One of the most effective ways to prevent burnout is by integrating play and creativity into your life. Play doesn't have to be reserved for children—adults benefit from unstructured, fun activities that engage the mind and body in new ways.

- **Examples of Play:** Whether it's engaging in a hobby like painting, playing a sport, or spending time outdoors, incorporating playful activities into your routine can reduce stress and improve overall well-being.
- **The Role of Creativity:** Creativity isn't just about artistic expression—it's about allowing your mind to explore new ideas and possibilities. Creative activities, such as journaling, drawing, or brainstorming, provide a break from the structured systems and routines you've built, allowing your mind to recharge.

By giving yourself time for play and creativity, you prevent burnout and ensure that your progress remains enjoyable.

2. Setting Boundaries

To sustain progress, you need to protect your time and energy by setting boundaries. Without clear boundaries, it's easy for work, personal obligations, and social commitments to encroach on your time, leaving you feeling overwhelmed.

- **How to Set Boundaries:** Be clear about your priorities and communicate them to others. If a certain time of day is reserved for personal projects or family time, protect it from interruptions. Setting boundaries helps you stay focused and ensures that you have time for rest and recovery.

Reflecting on Your Journey

As you work to sustain effortless progress, it's important to periodically reflect on your journey. Reflection allows you to see how far you've come, what you've learned, and how your mindset has evolved. It also gives you the opportunity to reconnect with your purpose and ensure that your goals are still aligned with your values.

1. Celebrate Milestones

Take time to celebrate the milestones you've achieved. Whether you've reached a major goal or simply maintained consistency, acknowledging your progress reinforces your efforts and motivates you to keep going.

- **Personal Milestones:** Reflect on the habits, systems, or routines that you've mastered. Celebrate how they've positively impacted your life.
- **Professional Milestones:** Consider the growth you've experienced in your career or business. Celebrate the wins, big and small, and the lessons learned along the way.

2. Realign with Your Purpose

As you grow and evolve, your goals and priorities may shift. Take time to periodically reflect on your purpose and ensure that your efforts are aligned with what truly matters to you. This reflection will help you stay focused on the goals that bring the most fulfillment and meaning.

Conclusion: A Life of Effortless Progress

Sustaining effortless progress is about building a life that feels aligned, intentional, and fulfilling. It's about creating systems that support your growth, habits that drive consistent action, and a mindset that embraces simplicity and long-term achievement.

The journey you've taken through this book has shown you that progress doesn't have to be a struggle. When you simplify your decisions, manage your time effectively, build systems that work for you, and sustain long-term habits, success becomes an inevitable outcome.

As you move forward, remember that the key to sustaining effortless progress is balance. It's about striving for growth while allowing room for rest, reflection, and adaptability. By staying true to the principles of simplicity and focus, you'll create a life where progress flows naturally and effortlessly.

Ultimately, this journey is about more than just reaching goals—it's about enjoying the process of growth and creating a life that feels aligned with your deepest values. With the tools, strategies, and systems you've built, you're well on your way to sustaining a life of simplicity and achievement.

10: Further Reading and Academic References

If you're eager to dive deeper into the principles of effortless progress, simplicity, systems thinking, and strategies for overcoming common obstacles, the following books, research, and resources offer additional insights, evidence, and practical strategies to support your journey.

Further Reading

These books provide actionable insights that complement the strategies discussed in this book, helping you continue your journey towards simplicity and sustainable success:

1. Atomic Habits by James Clear

This bestselling book delves into the power of tiny habits and how they can compound into significant change. Clear's actionable advice on habit formation aligns with the principles of effortless progress, helping you build routines that stick.

2. Deep Work by Cal Newport

In a world full of distractions, Cal Newport's *Deep Work* offers valuable strategies for creating focused, distraction-free time to produce meaningful work. His insights on time management and focus complement the time mastery techniques discussed in this book.

3. The Power of Habit by Charles Duhigg

Charles Duhigg's exploration of how habits are formed and changed provides a research-backed look at the psychology behind habits. His concept of the "habit loop" is essential for understanding how to create long-lasting behaviors.

4. Essentialism: The Disciplined Pursuit of Less by Greg McKeown

McKeown's book emphasizes the importance of focusing on what truly matters and eliminating distractions. *Essentialism* is a perfect companion for those looking to simplify their lives and focus on meaningful progress.

5. The ONE Thing by Gary Keller and Jay Papasan

This book explores the power of focusing on the single most important task at any given time to make exponential progress. Keller's message of simplicity and focus resonates with the core principles of effortless progress.

6. Getting Things Done by David Allen

David Allen's *Getting Things Done* methodology is a classic in time management. His approach to organizing tasks and eliminating overwhelm through simple systems is highly relevant to the systems-based approach advocated in this book.

7. Flow: The Psychology of Optimal Experience by Mihaly Csikszentmihalyi

Flow explores the concept of being fully immersed in a task and achieving peak performance. Understanding the flow state can help you find more ease and satisfaction in your work, making progress feel truly effortless.

8. The Art of Simplicity by Dominique Loreau

For those looking to apply the concept of simplicity beyond work and into their personal lives, *The Art of Simplicity* offers practical tips on minimalist living and focusing on what brings you joy.

Academic References

The following research studies provide the scientific foundation for many of the principles explored in this book, particularly in relation to common obstacles such as time management, decision fatigue, habit formation, and growth mindset.

1. Baumeister, R. F., & Tierney, J. (2011). *Willpower: Rediscovering the Greatest Human Strength.*

Baumeister's work on willpower and decision fatigue shows that making too many decisions depletes mental energy, leading to poorer quality decisions later in the day. This concept is foundational to simplifying decision-making processes, as explored in Chapter 2 and Chapter 7.

2. Pencavel, J. (2014). *The Productivity of Working Hours, The Economic Journal.*

Research from Stanford University revealed that productivity drops significantly when individuals work beyond 50 hours a week, with virtually no productivity gains past 55 hours. This supports the book's argument that hustle culture is inefficient for long-term success.

3. Lally, P., van Jaarsveld, C. H., Potts, H. W., & Wardle, J. (2010). *How are habits formed: Modelling habit formation in the real world, European Journal of Social Psychology.*

This study found that it takes, on average, 66 days to form a new habit, and the automaticity of a behavior grows with repetition. This research underscores the importance of consistent habits and routine, which is a central theme in Chapter 6 and Chapter 7.

4. Csikszentmihalyi, M. (1990). *Flow: The Psychology of Optimal Experience.*

Csikszentmihalyi's work on the concept of "flow" demonstrates how deep engagement in meaningful tasks leads to peak performance and satisfaction, aligning with the book's emphasis on focused, deep work in Chapter 3.

5. Lim, J., & Dinges, D. F. (2010). *A meta-analysis of the impact of short-term sleep deprivation on cognitive variables, Psychological Bulletin.*

This meta-analysis highlights the negative effects of sleep deprivation on attention, working memory, and decision-making, supporting the idea that rest and recovery are essential to sustaining effortless progress, as discussed in Chapter 7.

6. Grawitch, M. J., & Barber, L. K. (2013). *Workplace practices and employee outcomes: The role of psychological need satisfaction, Journal of Organizational Behavior.*

This study shows how time management techniques, such as time blocking and prioritization, improve employee well-being and productivity, emphasizing that focused work is more productive than multitasking.

7. Iyengar, S. S., & Lepper, M. R. (2000). *When choice is demotivating: Can one desire too much of a good thing? Journal of Personality and Social Psychology.*

This seminal study on choice overload found that too many choices can lead to decision paralysis and decreased satisfaction, highlighting the benefits of reducing options and simplifying decisions, which aligns with strategies discussed in Chapter 2 and Chapter 7.

8. Dweck, C. S. (2006). *Mindset: The New Psychology of Success.*

Carol Dweck's research on growth mindset versus fixed mindset is crucial for overcoming obstacles like setbacks and perfectionism, as discussed in Chapter 7. Those with a growth mindset are more likely to persist in the face of challenges, which is essential for sustaining progress.

9. American Society of Training and Development (2016). *Goal-Setting and Accountability Research*.

This study found that individuals who commit to goals with external accountability are significantly more likely to achieve them. The principle of external accountability is explored in Chapter 7 as a solution to inconsistent motivation.

Made in the USA
Columbia, SC
29 September 2024